the EDIBLE FLOWER GARDEN

Rosalind Creasy

PERIPLUS EDITIONS

Singapore • Hong Kong • Indonesia

First published in 1999 by Periplus Editions (HK) Ltd.

www.periplus.com

Photographs and text copyright © 1999 Rosalind Creasy,
except p 49 (*top*); Gudi Riter
Illustrations by Marcie Hawthorne

Library of Congress Cataloging-in-Publication Data

Creasy, Rosalind.
    The edible flower garden / by Rosalind Creasy.—1st ed.
         106 p. : ill. (some col.) ; 28 cm.
    Includes bibliographical references (p.)
    ISBN-10: 962-593-293-3 (paper); ISBN-13: 978-962-593-293-4
    1. Flower gardening. 2. Flowers. 3. Plants, Edible. 4. Cookery
(Flowers)   I. Title.
  SB405.C765 1999
  635.9—dc21   98036999
                            CIP

Distributed by:

NORTH AMERICA,
LATIN AMERICA & EUROPE
Tuttle Publishing
364 Innovation Drive
North Clarendon, VT 05759-9436 U.S.A
Tel: 1 (802) 773-8930
Fax: 1 (802) 773-6993
info@tuttlepublishing.com
www.tuttlepublishing.com

ASIA-PACIFIC
Berkeley Books Pte. Ltd.
3 Kallang Sector #04-01
Singapore 349278
Tel: (65) 6741-2178
Fax: (65) 6741-2179
inquiries@periplus.com.sg
www.tuttlepublishing.com

JAPAN
Tuttle Publishing
Yaekari Building, 3rd Floor
5-4-12 Osaki, Shinagawa-ku
Tokyo 141-0032
Tel: (81) 3 5437-0171
Fax: (81) 3 5437-0755
sales@tuttle.co.jp
www.tuttle.co.jp

First edition
23 22 21   10 9 8 7

Design by Kathryn Sky-Peck

Printed in China   2107EP

contents

contents

edible flower gardens

I t's incredible how many flowers or parts of flowers I've eaten in the past few years—lavender petals made into ice cream, zucchini blossoms stuffed with ricotta cheese, roses used in butter, to name just a few. And I've made an effort to share the experience, serving unsuspecting guests unadorned pineapple guava petals and an Art Deco–style cake with candied pansies. Not only do I eat edible flowers, but I've become a missionary in promoting them!

I'd love to be able to tell you about the first flower I ever ate, but I can't remember what it was. It was probably a nasturtium, though, eaten nearly twenty years ago. I'm certain I started slowly, since to eat flowers seemed odd to me, maybe even taboo. I remember eating rice garnished with calendula petals in Vermont and thinking that they made the dish colorful but didn't

add much to the flavor. Later I tried a few pansy petals served in a restaurant salad and still wasn't won over. It wasn't until I tasted lavender ice cream at an herb seminar that I became really enthusiastic. It was fantastic! I determined there and then to learn more about edible flowers.

Since that time I've probably asked everyone I know to eat flowers. A few people just plunge right in with delight, as if I've given them permission to enjoy a new pleasure. But most people are much more hesitant. One friend would accept my dinner invitation only after warning, "But I won't try any of your darn flowers!" You'd have thought I was offering her fried caterpillars. I've tried to get people to explain their hesitation about eating flowers, but they seem to have a hard time doing so. I certainly have difficulty explaining my initial reluctance. Why do others? Is it because we hesitate to try any new food? Somewhat. Is it a concern about the safety of eating them?

Edible flowers can be tucked into almost any garden scene. Here (left), pansies, roses, and chrysanthemums grow in my back garden. A bouquet of edible flowers (above) includes calendulas, scarlet runner beans, lavender, nasturtiums, and chive blossoms. The photo spread on pages 2 and 3 shows a sunny border designed for a client. I interspersed the edible roses, nasturtiums, and marigolds among the nonedible lantanas and plumbagos. I used their blue and lavender blooms to tone down the fiery reds and oranges.

Maybe. But I've just about concluded that, mainly, people believe that flowers are almost magical, so beautiful that only the eyes should feast on them. To those folks, eating flowers seems a bit greedy.

I've read everything I could find about edible flowers. I've asked every chef I've interviewed about his or her experiences with them. And I've tasted, tasted, and tasted every edible flower I could get my hands on, even stooping on occasion to sneak a bite of my hostess's centerpiece.

I've found the information available on edible flowers to be a strange hodgepodge. Much of our knowledge about edible flowers comes from old herbals. But when I turned to the herbals themselves, my confusion mounted. Eating flowers was commonplace in medieval Europe, when food often had a medicinal as well as a nutritional purpose. Sometimes the old recipes included dangerous flowers. Thus, a dish might call for two or three blossoms of foxglove, which is classified as poisonous today. True, we use foxglove to make digitalis, a heart stimulant, but only in carefully measured doses. I realized, as I read the old recipes, that the term *poisonous* is relative.

Displays of edible flowers (*right*) at farmer's market and exhibitions such as this one at the Tasting of Summer Produce in Oakland, California, get more sophisticated every year. On display are fuchsias, Johnny-jump-ups, tuberous begonias, nasturtiums, and rose petals. Flower petal confetti (*far right*) is a versatile little pleasure. Prior to serving, it can be sprinkled over an entree plate, a salad, or pastries.

4

As if the herbals' folk-medicine approach didn't make it difficult enough to determine which flowers are safe to eat, our forebears often called flowers by different names. For instance, what we know as calendula they called marigold; what we call cottage pink was gillyflower. So I was faced with the challenge of making sure the flowers referred to in the recipes matched the flowers we grow today.

And then which of the edible flowers are palatable? I collected a number of modern lists of edible flowers and cautiously began my taste testing. Some were absolutely horrible! Obviously, no one had tasted them before adding them to the lists. For example, some marigolds have a slightly lemony taste, others are tasteless, but the taste of most falls somewhere between skunk and quinine. Furthermore, none of these lists gave much guidance on *how* to eat the different kinds of flow-ers. I remember innocently putting an entire mullein petal into my mouth and finding it to be horribly astringent. I had the same experience with a car-nation petal. Later I learned that you need to first remove the terrible-tasting white part at the base of the petals.

Flowers should become a perma-nent part of our cuisine. They offer another alternative to salt and sugar as seasonings. Not only do flowers make those fruits and vegetables we want to increase in our diets, but their aesthetic value as decoration is obvious.

In researching this book, I asked every gardener, chef, and food expert I could talk to how they prepared edible flowers. And I arranged for a few edible flower gardens to be grown for this project: one by Carole Saville, an herb specialist in Los Angeles; another by the folks at the Chez Panisse restau-rant in Berkeley, California; not to mention my own little edible flower gardens.

If you're still hesitant about jumping in and growing an edible flower garden, I urge you to read along for inspiration. I bet that by the time you finish the cooking section, the sheer anticipation of working with flowers in your kitchen will have you planning your edible flower garden.

This harvest of edible flowers (*left*) is held by Judy Dornstroek. She and her husband grow edible flowers in their Pennsylvania greenhouse to sell to restaurants. Included are pink rose-scented geraniums, borage flowers, and nasturtiums of many colors. A harvest from my garden (*below, top*) includes broccoli and mustard blossoms, violets, violas, Johnny-jump-ups, the tiny maché flowers, calendulas, and nasturtiums. Edible flowers also can be used in bouquets. Here is a striking orange and blue bouquet from my garden (*below, bottom*) with lots of nasturtiums and the nonedible bachelor buttons.

Edible flowers can be found in all sorts of landscape situations. Chestnut roses (*left*) grace a front yard in Jackson, Mississippi. Nasturtiums (*above*, *top*) cascade out of a planter and complement the Spanish architecture in a California garden. In New Jersey, many varieties of scented geraniums (*above*, *bottom*) line a walk at Well-Sweep Herb Farm.

how to grow edible flowers

All sorts of plants produce edible flowers, but it's the annual flowers—those that are seeded, grown, and produce all in just one season, like nasturtiums, pansies, and squash blossoms—that people are most familiar with. The easiest way to obtain edible flowers is to inventory the plants already growing in your garden.

First, peruse the Encyclopedia of Edible Flowers (page 29) to see which plants produce edible flowers; then walk around your property to see which ones you have. Be sure to check out your vegetable garden too, as some of those plants produce great flowers.

Then, before you go any further, get acquainted with the accompanying poisonous plant list (pages 14–15). To make sure you properly identify the flowers, please obtain a couple of basic field guides to edible plants (see the Bibliography, page 104). And just to be safe, you might take a sample of whatever you are considering eating to a local nursery for a positive identification.

Once you have inventoried your landscape for flowering "delicacies," consider adding a few choice perennials, bulbs, shrubs, or trees. Daylilies, tulips, roses, and apple blossoms, for example, all have edible flowers. Because they grow for years—perenni-ally—such plants need a permanent site; consider carefully where to locate them.

Perennials are generally planted from divisions or from grafted plant material, depending on the species, and they need good soil preparation and drainage, though they are usually not

My back patio edible flower garden (*right*) was designed with pink in mind. The flowers are a combination of annuals and perennials. A miniature pink rose sits in a container, and the perennial Alpine strawberries, English daisies, pinks, and day lilies fill in most of the bed. I supplement the beds with pansies in the spring and chrysanthemums in the fall.

as fussy about soil fertility and moisture as annual flowers and vegetables are. For more information on planting perennials, see Appendix A, "Planting and Maintenance" (page 92).

Most of the plants that produce edible flowers need at least six hours of sun each day. Add perennial edible flowers to your landscape easily by installing a border of lavender plants along a driveway; putting in a small sitting area surrounded by daylilies and chrysanthemums; adding a little herb corner off the patio planted with

Carole Saville (*top*) helps plant my nasturtium garden. One year, I planted a whole garden of nasturtiums (*below*) and trialed a dozen varieties. Here, Jody Main and Adam Lane harvest handfuls of blooms from that garden. The nasturtiums all tasted the same, but the color variations were fantastic.

All herb flowers (*above*) are edible. Consequently, an herb garden is a great place to find more flowers for your salad. Here, my streetside herb border contains nepitella (Italian mint), lavender, and lemon thyme, all herbs that produce flowers. Not all herbs bloom, however. Included in the bed are variegated oregano and sage, which never produce flowers. For a larger selection of edible flowers, I added blue and yellow violas and pansies to the herb planting.

sage, chives, fennel, and bee balm; or planting more than your usual number of tulips in the fall. If you're feeling a little more ambitious, plant a redbud or apple tree to give you privacy from a neighbor's window. Maybe you've always wanted a lilac; now you have one more excuse to plant one. By adding just a few plants here and there, you can add quite a bit to your repertoire in the kitchen.

The Encyclopedia of Edible Flowers (page 29) details which varieties produce the best edible flowers and provides information on growing all the plants mentioned—enough to get you started and give you an idea of how much care the plants need. Occasionally you may need to consult other books for different information—local cultivars or conditions, for example. Be aware that the authors of most of the flower-culture books in this country do not anticipate your eating the flowers and therefore occasionally recommend pesticides that are unsafe for human consumption. (Nontoxic, organic pest and disease controls are given in Appendix B, Pest and Disease Control, page 99.)

Unlike vegetable varieties, the flowers bred at nurseries have been selected not for their flavor but for their ap-

pearance and growing ease. Therefore, taste as many varieties as possible before you plant. Visit the gardens of friends and neighbors and taste a few flowers at a time. *But beware of poisons!* Before you start tasting flowers, let alone planning your garden, you need a brief lesson on poisonous plants.

Poisonous Plants

What is poisonous, anyway? When I began my research I was naive enough to assume that I would be able to find a definitive list of poisonous flowering plants. No such luck. There are plenty of lists of poisonous plants, but none that completely resolves the issue of what is and is not poisonous. I had to do my own legwork, so I began at the beginning, with *Webster's Third: poison:*

"A substance . . . that in suitable quanti-ties has properties harmful or fatal to an organism when it is brought into contact with or absorbed by the organism."

So the two crucial factors are chemi-cal contents and dosage. As to the for-mer, plants containing alkaloids, glyco-sides, resins, alcohols, phenols, and oxalates are potentially poisonous, but their toxicity depends on the amount of these substances they contain. After all, many poisonous plants are also valuable medicines; it is the dosage that determines whether the end product is medicinal or toxic. In fact, some poisonous-plant lists actually include spinach and chard because they contain oxalic acid, which is poisonous in large quantities.

Still, determining how much of a substance makes a plant or serving toxic is a matter for chemists. Obviously, the more you ingest—eat-ing foxglove ice cream rather than just a single petal on a salad plate—the greater the hazard. My advice and the rule I follow is, Don't take chances. If a flowering plant is on *any* list of poison-ous plants, I don't eat it—not even a single petal—until I have more infor-mation. And if I can't find the plant on any list of *edible* or poisonous plants, I assume it is *not* edible.

Here are some guidelines I have gathered from food technologists and environmental botanists:

1. Positively identify the plant—Latin name and all. As with mushrooms, identification is crucial.

2. Birds and animals are unharmed by some plants that are poisonous to humans. The gray squirrel can safely eat the deadly amanita mushroom, and birds regularly gorge on the irri-tating red elderberry berries. So don't depend on guinea pigs of any species to guide you.

3. Not all parts of toxic plants are nec-essarily poisonous. For instance, rhubarb stalks and potatoes are edible, but the leaves of both plants are poiso-nous.

4. Some plants, such as pokeweed, are poisonous only at certain times of the year.

5. Because individuals can be allergic to substances that are not generally poisonous—wheat and milk, for example—when you first taste a new food, eat only a small amount.

6. Just because most members of a par-ticular plant family are not poisonous does not mean that all are.

7. Heating or cooking in water removes many toxins, but not all.

8. Never use any flower as a garnish if it's not edible. In this day and age, when diners eat flowers, you're just asking for an accidental poisoning.

9. Make sure it's clear to children that some flowers are edible and others can make them sick.

10. And a most important point: You can cause damage and not even know it. Because a plant does not make you sick to your stomach or cause your heart to race or make you break out in a rash doesn't mean that it's safe. Some toxic reactions take time to manifest them-selves; others will never be detected. For example, some plants contain chemicals that cause cancer, abortions, or birth defects; others are filled with chemicals that raise your blood pressure, rob the body of calcium, or tie up iron.

Below is a list of a few of the most common poisonous plants and the parts of the plants known to be dan-gerous.

Amaryllis *Hippeastrum puniceum*: Bulb
Anemone *Anemone tuberosa* and other spp: All
Autumn Crocus *Colchicum autumnale*: All

Azalea *Rhododendron spp.*: All

Belladonna Lily (Naked Lady)
    Amaryllis belladonna: Bulb

Bird-of-Paradise *Strelitzia reginae*:
    Seeds and pods

Buckeye (Horse Chestnut) *Aesculus
    arguta* and *A. hippocastanum* and
    other spp.: Seeds, flowers, and leaves

Buttercup *Ranunculus* spp.: All

Caladium *Caladium bicolor* and other
    spp.: All

Cardinal Flower *Lobelia cardinalis*:
    Particularly the bulb

Clematis *Clematis*: All

Daffodil *Narcissus pseudonarcissus*:
    Particularly the bulb

Datura *Datura meteloides*: All

Delphinium *Delphinium* spp.: All

Foxglove *Digitalis purpurea*: All

Gloriosa Lily *Gloriosa* spp.: All

Hydrangea *Hydrangea* spp.: All

Iris *Iris* spp.: Leaves and rootstock

Jessamine *Gelsemium sempervirens:* All

Lantana *Lantana* spp.: All

Larkspur *Delphinium* spp.: All

Lily-of-the-Valley *Convallaria majalis*:
    All

Lupine *Lupinus* spp.: All

Monkshood *Aconitum* spp.: All

Narcissus *Narcissus* spp.: All

Oleander *Nerium oleander:* All

Poinsettia *Euphorbia pulcherrima*: All

Most landscapes contain both edible and nonedible flowers. It's important for children in particular to be taught the difference. Here, edible roses, society garlic, and nasturtiums grow among the nonedible coreopsis and iris.

Rhododendron *Rhododendron* spp.: All

Star-of-Bethlehem *Ornithogalum* spp.:
    All

Sweet Pea *Lathyrus* spp.: All

Tansy *Tanacetum vulgare:* All

Wisteria *Wisteria floribunda* and *W.
    sinensis:* Pods and seeds

my edible flower gardens

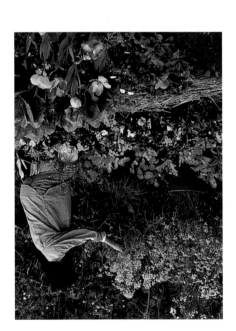

My front walk (*right*) is festooned with edible flowers, including roses, winter savory, society garlic, the species marigolds 'Lemon Gem,' and 'Empress of India' nasturtiums.

always have edible flowers growing in my yard. Some (lavender, daylilies, and anise hyssop) grow in ornamental flower borders, others (rosemary and thyme) are part of my herb corner, and still others (squash and broccoli) grow in the vegetable garden. Sometimes, though, just for fun I like to try new edible flower varieties or illustrate how little room it takes to grow a selection of flowers for the kitchen, so I grow tiny gardens of only edible flowers.

It never stops amazing me how little the space it takes to grow an enormous number and variety of blossoms for the table. The garden illustrated on pages 18–19 was located in my front-yard vegetable garden and included eleven species of edible flowers—enough to make a huge impact in the kitchen. I chose yellow, orange, and blue flowers. The total area of this little flower garden was six feet by twelve feet with a two-foot-wide path running through the middle, or about sixty square feet of bed space. As it turned out, half that size would have been plenty.

I live in a mild-winter area, so I planted my garden in early fall. Gardeners in USDA Zones 1 through 8 would plant this type of garden in the spring, starting many of the plants in flats six weeks before the average last frost date. I planted the mizuna, arugula, nasturtiums, and calendulas directly in the garden from seeds. The rest of the plants came from a nursery. My soil is in enviable condition after twenty years of soil building, so I didn't need to add amendments at planting time. First, I laid out the beds. Because they are the tallest, I filled the back

One year, I took the middle two beds out of my vegetable garden and planted them primarily with annual edible flowers. In spring, these little plots produced enough flowers to decorate a panoply of fancy platters. The drawing (*above*) indicates the location of the plants. In the back row, the north side of the garden (*to the left*), I planted the tallest plants so they would not shade the shorter species. The back row contains (*top to bottom*) arugula and mizuna (a Japanese mustard). The next row contains yellow nasturtiums and a chive plant, orange calendulas, and red and orange nasturtiums. The front row contains yellow and lavender violas and 'Antique' mix pansies. Across the path (*top to bottom*), are romaine lettuces, yellow violas, white English daisies, Alpine strawberries, and the red lettuce 'Lolla Rossa.' In the middle is a cluster of

tulips, and the front row was planted with bunching onions, purple violas, and more English daisies.

row of one bed with arugula and mizuna, a Japanese-type mustard. The middle row contained nasturtiums and calendulas, which grow to about eighteen inches. In the front row I planted the shorter pansies, violas, Johnny-jump-ups. In another bed I included strawberries, pansies, English daisies, and tulips as well as half a dozen heads of romaine and frilly red lettuces and a cluster of bunching onions—all great for salads. I could have included cilantro, fennel,

radishes, bush peas, broccoli, and many more types of mustard, but I planted them in the vegetable garden that year because I like to rotate crops.

Over the years I have noticed that the cool-weather edible flowers are the savory ones that are great for salads, appetizers, and garnishes for winter and spring meals. The sweet flowers on roses, lavender, honeysuckle, and scented geraniums all bloom in warm weather. That winter I was able to harvest pansies, violas, Johnny-jump-

ups, and calendulas—all great for sal-ads and garnishes—from early winter through late spring. Our frosts knocked out my nasturtiums, so I replanted them in early spring. Soon the tulips, English daisies, mizuna, and the arugula came into their glory. I could now make an even greater range of appetizers and butters and fancier salads. In the middle of spring the nasturtiums kicked in and the strawberries started to flower (and

My little annual edible flower garden (left) in early spring produced tulips, violas, mustard flowers, and a few English daisies. A few weeks later, the same garden was in full swing (above) and the violas and nasturtiums were exuberant, growing in among each other, as were the chives, pansies, and calendulas.

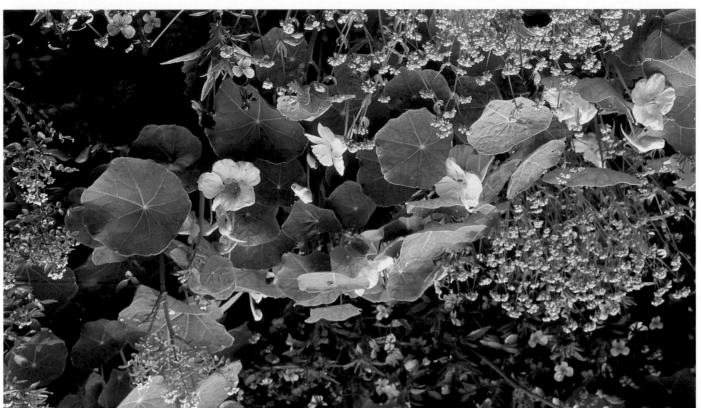

kept going through the summer). In late spring the chives came into bloom, the English daisies were starting to dwindle, and the mizuna went to seed and were pulled out. A few weeks later I needed to pull out most of the plants in order to plant summer vege-tables. If I had the space to allow most of the edible flower plants to go to seed (as I do some years), the nastur-tiums, arugula, Johnny-jump-ups, calendulas, and mizuna would have reseeded themselves and the next fall very little planting would have been needed to renew the beds (the straw-berries, chives, and English daisies are perennials).

I planted another edible flower gar-den off my back patio (see page 11). It had a completely different color scheme: burgundy pansies, pink dianthus, light yellow 'Stella de Oro' dwarf daylilies, primrose yellow nasturtiums, Alpine strawberries, baby-pink roses, and var-iegated society garlic. Probably the most dramatic and fun edible flower garden I ever created was one planted with only nasturtiums—ten different varieties, to be exact (see page 12). It was eye-opening to see how many different varieties there were. Some were double, others were bicolored, and still others had green and white foliage. Of course, it produced a "gazil-lion" nasturtiums, and everyone who visited left with a big enough bouquet to cook with for a week.

Many edible flowers will reseed themselves like crazy. This little corner of my garden (below) grows by itself. Every spring it is completely filled with Johnny-jump-ups, nasturtiums, mâche, and watercress with its edible lacy white blossoms shown on the right.

The Chez Panisse Flower Garden

A number of years ago I invited Andrea Crawford, then manager of the Chez Panisse restaurant garden in Berkeley, California, to join me in an experiment: growing a prototypical edible flower garden with which the chefs could experiment. She and Alice Waters, the executive chef of Chez Panisse, had been growing and serving edible flowers for years and were eager to learn even more. In this garden we grew flowers that none of us had ever

used in the kitchen before.

To begin, we looked over my list of edible flowers, perused seed catalogs for unusual varieties, and ordered a good selection. Both Andrea and I gathered information from everyone we knew who had grown our selec-tions. Jan Blüm, of Seeds Blüm, sent us 'Fragrance' dianthus seeds; Renee Shepherd, of Renee's Garden, sent us 'Kablouna' calendula, anise hyssop, and 'Whirlybird' nasturtium seeds; and we both raided our own supplies of seeds and plants. We concentrated mainly on annual flowers because we

wanted to evaluate the flowers in the kitchen within a year and because they are easiest for most gardeners to obtain. Andrea had been producing borage, Johnny-jump-ups, lavender, climbing nasturtiums, violas, mustard, radishes, chicory, scented geraniums, and herbs for the restaurant, and she chose varieties from among her favor-ites. For years I had been growing scarlet runner beans, English daisies, and marigolds, but I had never tasted their flowers and was curious about them, so I chose the most promising varieties. I also selected 'Empress of India' and 'Alaska' nasturtiums, two particular varieties I had never used in the kitchen.

Summertime temperatures in Berkeley are moderated by morning fog, and few days exceed 90°F. The winters are mild, with temperatures seldom dropping below freezing.

Though you might be hesitant at first about trying to duplicate much of this garden if you live in a northern region, almost all the flowers can actually be grown equally well anywhere in the country. The soil in the Berkeley gar-den was clay with a tremendous amount of organic matter added. The beds were in wonderful shape after years of loving care. Andrea, like most good gardeners, is passionate about soil preparation, and her years of effort

Andrea Crawford (left) and Alice Waters com-pare notes on the edible flowers growing in the Chez Panisse garden. A harvest of edible flowers (right) from the Chez Panisse garden includes hollyhocks, squash blossom, nastur-tiums, 'Lemon Gem' marigolds, calendulas, runner beans, and gladiolas.

showed. Her garden received no rain from May through September, and summer watering was a constant necessity.

Andrea and I sat down to discuss both her experiences in the garden and the chefs' experiences in the kitchen. She was eager to sum it all up. She reminded me that she and Alice had been planning a pansy garden for the restaurant and had already planted flats. It had seemed natural to add hollyhocks, scarlet runner beans, anise hyssop, Austrian Copper roses, 'Adnami' chrysanthemums, Alpine strawberries, and 'Lemon Gem' marigolds and to make the new, expanded garden both an ornamental border and a productive garden. We agreed to try to grow the approximate amounts a home gardener would use. "Well," said Andrea, "we planted far more than a person could ever use at home. In fact, that narrow strip, which is thirty feet by two and a half feet, produced more than the restaurant could use; but we viewed the beds as an ornamental garden that a person could also eat out of, and that was really very nice."

Andrea reported that Stokes Seeds had the best selection and that she could get just about all the varieties she needed from them. Thompson & Morgan, on the other hand, turned out to be really frustrating. They offered a large number of varieties, but Andrea found that they often seemed to be out of what she wanted and sent back credit slips instead of seeds.

In the end, the most successful and versatile edible flowers were the species Andrea had always grown for the restaurant—the nasturtiums, borage, and calendulas. Of the new flowers planted, the pansies—all varieties—were probably the most useful and were a lot of fun as well. The chefs used them as garnishes and chopped them into butters. The anise hyssop

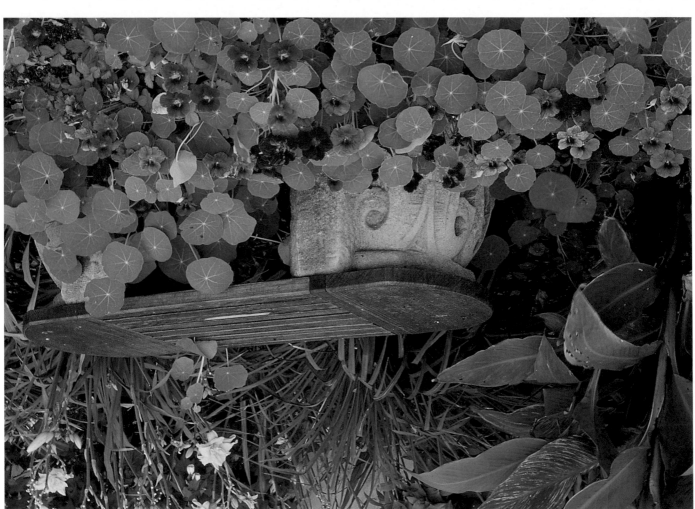

Nasturtiums and daylilies frame a garden bench.

was very flavorful. The runner blossoms were tasty too—the chefs mixed them with other flowers and put them in salads. "Of the nasturtiums," Andrea told me, "we liked 'Alaska' and 'Empress of India.' The flowers of these varieties are similar to those of most other varieties, but the leaves are beautiful, and when they are small they are quite delicious. We hadn't used those before. With nasturtiums, taste is the most important factor, and that's affected by how you grow them. If you start them without much water, they're quite hot to the taste. They grow best in really lush conditions, and then they're much milder."

On the other hand, the hollyhocks were a complete failure—they didn't have much flavor and had a slippery quality like that of okra. Still, Andrea thought they might be good dipped in batter and fried tempura-style. She went on to say, "Most of the calendulas we tried didn't impress me as much as our simple pot marigolds, which self-seed right here in the garden. They have large flowers and nothing seems to affect them. I don't like 'Kablouna,' because you can't get the petals off the tight head easily. And I found Stokes's claims about their calendulas—all these so-called scarlet, gold, and apricot tones—to be an overstatement. The differences among them are very subtle."

Andrea told me they did a lot of experimenting with the flowers in the kitchen. For example, she picked two deep tubs—that's probably about ten gallons— of nasturtium flowers. She then asked the chefs to get creative with them, and they made a soup with potatoes and the nasturtiums. According to Andrea, it was a total flop. "It was really awful," she said. "It had kind of a slimy texture. So we found out that you can't use nasturtiums in great quantities; they have to be used quite sparingly." Their most successful way of using nasturtiums was to chop them and mash the bits into butter. The butter then looks like it has been laced with confetti, especially when borage and pansies are chopped up along with the nasturtiums, to get blue and purple. "It's very pretty," said Andrea, "and you can put it on pasta, steak, or toast. Alice [Waters] also found this to be a good way to use flowers that have started to wilt. Squash blossoms, too, are wonderful. The chefs stuff them with cheese, or chop and fry them and serve them over pasta. They also sauté them with vegetables. Squash blossoms are very versatile and have a pleasant, delicate flavor."

Chez Panisse chefs use flowers not only in salads and butter but in many of their famous desserts. They put fresh flowers on cakes and soufflés or candy them and use them whole or chopped. The sugar makes the flowers sparkle. "Very pretty on a chocolate cake," Andrea said. "The chefs sprinkle it on the sides and then, using a small doily as a stencil over the top, make a little design all the way around of sparkling, multicolored glitter. This glitter idea came from using the delicate candied flowers. It turned out to be a great way to use the broken ones."

The chefs love to use the flowers as flavorings in ice cream. Before making the basic custard mix, they steep the petals in milk for as long as it takes to flavor it—anywhere from a few hours to a day, depending on the intensity they want. Then they strain out the flowers. They aim to flavor the custard slightly stronger than they want the end result, because some of the flavor gets lost during freezing. The most successful flower ice cream, and Andrea's personal favorite, is anise hyssop, but the chefs have made ice cream with everything from rose petals, lavender, and almond blossoms to many of the scented geraniums.

"Over the years," Andrea concluded, "we've found that you really have to think about how you use flowers. They should enhance the meal, not just be thrown randomly onto the plate or into the salad. The flower garnishes, for instance, need to have some relation to the food. So thyme flowers in a savory soup or chive blossoms in a salad instead of onion would be great, but just floating pansies by themselves on a soup doesn't make any sense.

"I would definitely grow all the edible flowers again, even the hollyhocks. They're so beautiful, and it's fun to share them with your friends. And there may be ways to use them that I just haven't discovered. I think having a flower border that's entirely edible is a good enough reason in itself to plant it. People who visit the restaurant are delighted with the edible flowers. All in all, it seems a great way to combine the beautiful flowers in the garden with what you enjoy on your table."

interview

Alice Waters

Alice Waters is the proprietor and inspiration behind one of this country's most famous and revolutionary restaurants, Chez Panisse, in Berkeley, California. Although I had worked with Alice casually over the years, I never appreciated her vast range of talent and knowledge until I interviewed her specifically about edible flowers. While other chefs can talk about *some* of the most common edible flowers, Alice expounds on *many* with an excitement that's infectious.

"How do patrons react to flowers on their plate?" I asked. "The flowers are a fascination," Alice said. "People really focus on them and are very curious. Some people refuse to eat them, but about half will taste them readily. I like to serve them in such a way that they're tasty and accessible to people; a large flower by itself is a little intimidating. I like to incorporate Johnny-jump-ups or nasturtium petals in salads—or serve them in ice cream or butter."

I gave Alice the list of edible flowers I had compiled and asked her to comment on those she had tried. Her face brightened as she perused the list; she seemed to be able to replay the tastes and feelings of those she had used.

"Calendulas have a real nice flavor," she began. "Not too strong, but kind of peppery—even a little grassy. I use fresh petals in salads, or I like to dry them and use them in soups in the winter. Honey-suckle is good too," she continued. "It's very sweet and tastes just like it smells; it's quite extraordinary in some desserts. You don't need much of it, though, just a little spoonful.

"Lavender is wonderful. You can use it in both sweet and savory dishes, as a marinade for meats, or for lavender ice cream. I'm crazy about nasturtiums too. 'Empress of India,' which has a dark red color, has a spicy, peppery flavor. I enjoy using the 'Alaska' variety in salads because the foliage is so beautiful—variegated green and white. I also use nasturtiums to top soups, salads, or pizzas—for example, smoked salmon pizza. Just put them on top at the last minute so they won't wilt. In butters, the colors and flavors seem suspended.

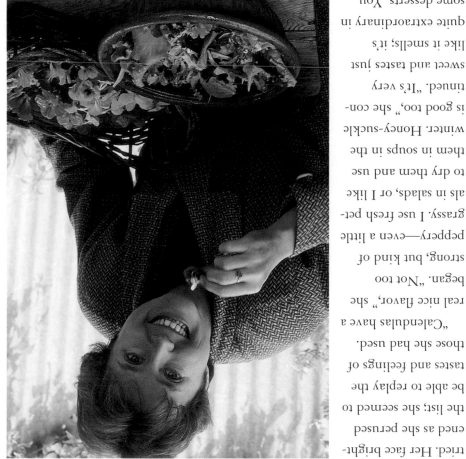

Alice Waters is proprietor of Chez Panisse Restaurant in Berkeley and one of the most influential chefs in the world of fresh produce.

"And certainly we have to talk about roses and violets. Rose petals are fantastic; they have all different flavors, depending on the variety. On one special occasion I used 'Damask' roses in ice cream and garnished it with deep red-orange 'Joseph's Coat' rose petals that had been dipped in egg white and sprinkled with sugar. Another time I chopped candied rose petals so they looked like little sparkles—very special. I find brightly colored varieties most effective. And we use fragrant violets in late winter; we candy them and then use them to garnish sherbets, or we fold fresh violets into ice cream just before we serve it."

The day I interviewed Alice, a gentleman from Texas called to find out if Chez Panisse was the restaurant that served edible flowers; he wanted to come try some. It seems that people are finding delight in trying new tastes, and Chez Panisse leads the way.

encyclopedia of edible
flowers

The following entries detail what I consider the most versatile edible flowers. The basic cultural information on preparing the soil, planting, seed starting, watering, mulching, fertilizing, pruning, and controlling pests and diseases are covered in Appendices A and B (pages 92–102).

You may notice that a few species occasionally sold as "edible" flowers—bachelor's buttons, impatiens, and snap dragons—are not listed. There is no evidence in any of the historical or scientific literature to indicate that they are edible. Why then are they regarded as edible? I've been able to trace it all back to an article published in the late

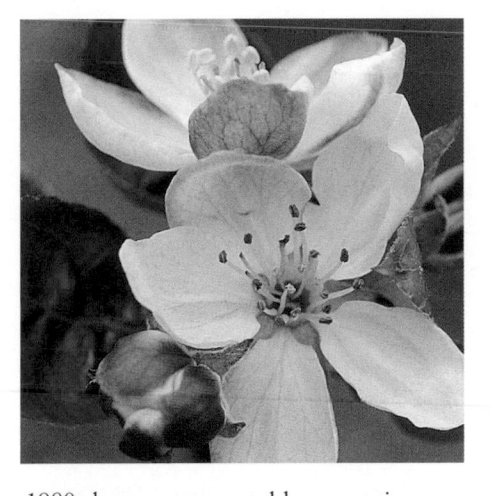

1980s by a very reputable magazine. Upon calling the editor to see where the author had obtained this information, I was shocked to learn that the list came from a young grower who "thought," but had no proof, that these

plants were edible. Two other flowers on that infamous list are stock and petunias. Although stock was eaten during famine in southern Europe, the question remains, Why didn't people eat stock at other times? Does it taste bad or does it have long-term side effects? According to Craig Dremann of the Redwood City Seed Company, the Andean Indians used petunias to induce a feeling of flight during their religious ceremonies. Not exactly what you want to feed your family. I also omitted primrose. There is an edible primrose, *Primula vera*, that is popular in England, but it is seldom ever grown in America.

English lavender and 'Alaska' nasturtiums (*left*) line my front walk. Apple blossoms (*above*) are fragrant and tasty spring treats.

ANISE HYSSOP

Agastache foeniculum

AN EXCEPTION IN THE HERB world in that it's native to the Western Hemisphere, anise hyssop is one of the most flavorful and interesting edible flowers.

How to grow: This highly orna-mental, easily grown herbaceous perennial reaches from 3 to 6 feet and has gray green leaves and striking, dense 1- to 3-inch flower spikes rang-ing from lavender to white. It is hardy to USDA Zone 4. Start anise hyssop from seeds or divisions, grow it in full sun in average soil, and keep it fairly moist. The plant dies down in the win-ter and often reseeds itself the next spring. It is bothered by few pests and diseases. Harvest flowers as they appear in the summer.

How to prepare: The young leaves and tiny petals of the sweet flowers have a flavor somewhat between anise and root beer and, if used sparingly, are very pleasant in both savory and sweet dishes. Add the petals to melted butter and serve over grilled mush-rooms, use them in a beef stir-fry or a chicken marinade, or include them in a salad dressing. The natural sweetness and many complex flavors give dimen-sion to iced drinks, custard, ice cream and sorbets, and pound cake. A few dried flower heads in the sugar bowl adds flavor to sugar for tea or sugar cookies. See the recipe for Stir-Fried Beef with Anise Hyssop on page 83.

Anise hyssop

'Pink Pearl' apple blossoms (*top*), 'Golden Delicious' apple blossoms (*left*), 'Red Delicious' apple blossoms (*right*)

APPLE BLOSSOMS

Malus spp.

APPLE TREES PERFUME THE AIR in spring and glorify the landscape. Capture their fragrance in your desserts.

How to grow: Most varieties of apple trees bear light pink to white flowers in early spring. 'Pink Pearl,' an old heirloom apple available from a few specialty fruit tree nurseries, bears deep pink blossoms. Buy apple trees bare root in late winter (which is when the trees are dormant with soil re-moved from their roots) and consult a good fruit-growing text for selecting and planting varieties appropriate for your area. Remember to keep the blos-soms free of heavy-duty chemical sprays.

How to prepare: Apple blossoms have a slightly floral taste; the petals are lovely in salads, especially a Waldorf salad, or in a cider vinaigrette. Infuse the petals in cream for ice cream or whipped cream to go over an apple tart. You can also crystallize the petals and use them to garnish baked apples drizzled with maple syrup, applesauce, tarts, fruit soups, and French toast or crêpes filled with caramelized apples.

'Grand Duke of Tuscany' Jasmine

ARABIAN JASMINE

Jasminum sambac

JASMINE INVOKES IMAGES of sultry evenings in faraway places.

How to grow: A tender perennial vine native to tropical Asia, Arabian jasmine is hardy only in USDA Zone 10. In all other areas, it can be grown indoors with high humidity in a greenhouse. There are two Arabian jasmine cultivars of merit: 'Grand Duke of Tuscany,' which has intensely perfumed double flowers and is slow growing, and 'Maid of Orleans,' a bushy, compact plant with semidouble-white flowers. They can be obtained from mail-order nurseries specializing in tropical plants. Outside, grow Arabian jasmine in full sun or partial shade in average soil, with average watering. It is a heavy feeder, so fertilize with fish emulsion every two weeks during the growing season. When the plants are about to flower, feed them cottonseed meal or some other form of phosphorus. They grow best in temperatures of 60°F at night and 80°F during the day. Harvest the flowers just as they open.

How to prepare: Use the flowers to infuse simple syrups or impart their lovely perfume to tea. Use the syrup as a wonderful base for sorbets or ice creams or pour it over melons, figs, or poached pears.

ARUGULA

Eruca vesicaria

ARUGULA FLOWERS ARE NUTTY and taste a bit like horseradish. Mellow and delightful, these flowers can be used in any dish that calls for arugula.

How to grow: Arugula is grown for its leaves; the flowers are a bonus. These cool-weather plants can be enjoyed in early spring and again in the fall. The plants are short-lived; they get quite spicy and go to flower readily in hot weather. Broadcast the seeds over rich soil in a sunny area and lightly cover them with soil, or start them in flats indoors. Keep arugula well watered and fertilize lightly. Arugula has few pest and disease problems. Harvest individual leaves when the plants are at least 4 inches tall, and the flowers as they appear. Arugula flowers attract beneficial insects, so I keep plants blooming for much of the spring. If allowed to go to seed, arugula reseeds itself readily in your garden.

How to prepare: Long after the leaves have become too strong-tasting to use, the flowers can still be sprinkled over green or pasta salads, slivered fennel, carpaccio, frittatas, and pizzas; tucked into sandwiches filled with tomatoes or grilled mushrooms and eggplants; minced and added to a soft cheese; and used to garnish chilled tomato soup and vegetables prepared with olive oil and garlic in the Italian manner.

arabian jasmine — arugula

BEE BALM

(Monarda, Oswego tea)

Monarda didyma, M. citriodora

BEE BALM, ALSO CALLED monarda, is an exuberant plant that is native to eastern North America. In earlier times Native Americans, and later the early settlers, used it to make tea.

How to grow: Bee balm produces 3-inch shaggy flowers over much of the summer. Of all the many varieties, the red cultivars seem to be the tastiest: 'Cambridge Scarlet,' 'Adam,' and 'Firecracker.' An annual monarda, 'Lamabata,' has lavender flowers and spicy petals that can be used sparingly in savory dishes, such as a green salad or cream soup, and as a garnish.

Obtain monarda plants from local nurseries and mail-order firms that specialize in perennials.

Bee balm is a hardy, easy-to-grow perennial that can get to 4 feet tall. Start it with divisions planted in sun or partial shade, in moist soil. Mildew is a common problem in many climates. Harvest flowers as they appear in summer.

How to prepare: The flowers of the red varieties of bee balm have a fairly strong, spicy, minty taste. They are most commonly used along with the leaves to make herbal tea. Add the petals to teas and salads; sprinkle them over red snapper or other mild fish; include them in dishes with apricots, peaches, and plums; use them in the punch bowl and in fruit salads or to garnish cold drinks; or add them to apple jelly and baked goods such as pound cake.

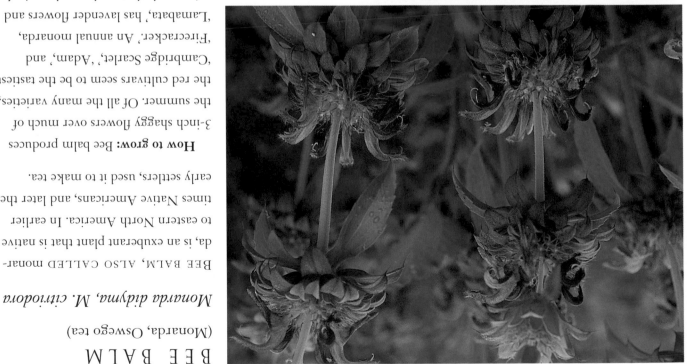

'Lamabata' monarda *(above)*, 'Cambridge Scarlet' *(left and inset)*

TUBEROUS BEGONIAS

Begonia X tuberhybridia

THESE SHOWY FLOWERS are sensational in the garden and on the table.

How to grow: Spectacular puffs of orange, yellow, white, pink, or red, tuberous begonia flowers range in size from 2 to 4 inches across. To ensure safe eating, either grow them without chemicals or buy chemicals that are registered for edible plants. In some climates tuberous begonias are prone to mildew, but in many cool-summer areas these plants grow with ease. Start begonia tubers in flats or pots in the spring in rich, moist, well-draining potting soil. When the plants are 3 inches high, replant them in the garden or in containers. They need a slightly acidic soil, filtered sun, and constant moisture and feeding. Dig up the tubers in late fall, knock off the dead and dying stalks, and store the tubers in a cool, dry, frost-free place. Do not lift the tubers until the foliage turns yellow.

How to prepare: The flowers of most tuberous begonias have a delicious, light, lemon taste and a crisp texture. Taste them before using them to make sure they are not astringent. Use sliced petals in salads and tea sandwiches. Dip whole petals in flavored yogurt and serve as an appetizer that is sure to spark a conversation. Garnish a fish plate or a fruit or green salad with begonia petals, or use them as a spectacular garnish on an appetizer platter for a buffet.

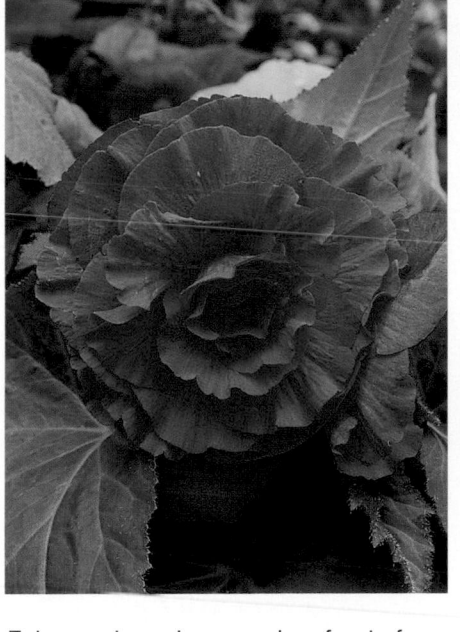

Tuberous begonias come in a feast of colors.

Borage flowers (*above*) are easy to harvest.

BORAGE

Borago officinalis

THIS HERB, NATIVE TO EUROPE and Africa, has a slight cucumber flavor. The special blue star-shaped flowers are lovely on salads and in cold drinks.

How to grow: An easily grown summer annual that sometimes acts like a biennial, borage grows to about 2 feet and has hairy gray leaves and half-inch star-shaped deep blue flowers. Borage is easily started from seeds planted in average soil and in full sun in the spring after any threat of frost is over. Harvest young leaves once the plants are established, and flowers anytime they appear. Borage often reseeds itself.

How to prepare: Mix the half-inch flowers in vegetable and fruit salads, especially a cucumber or jicama salad, or use them to garnish cream soups or to decorate desserts. Freeze them in ice cubes to float in iced tea. They can also be crystallized. To make the flowers edible, remove the hairy sepals using the following simple procedure. With your left hand (if you are right-handed) grasp the stem of the flower. With your right hand gently pinch the middle of the star and pull. The flower (corolla) should separate from the sepals intact.

Caution: Pregnant and lactating women should avoid borage flowers, as more than eight to ten flowers can cause milk to flow.

BROCCOLI
Brassica oleracea

BROCCOL RAAB
B. rapa (B. campestris)

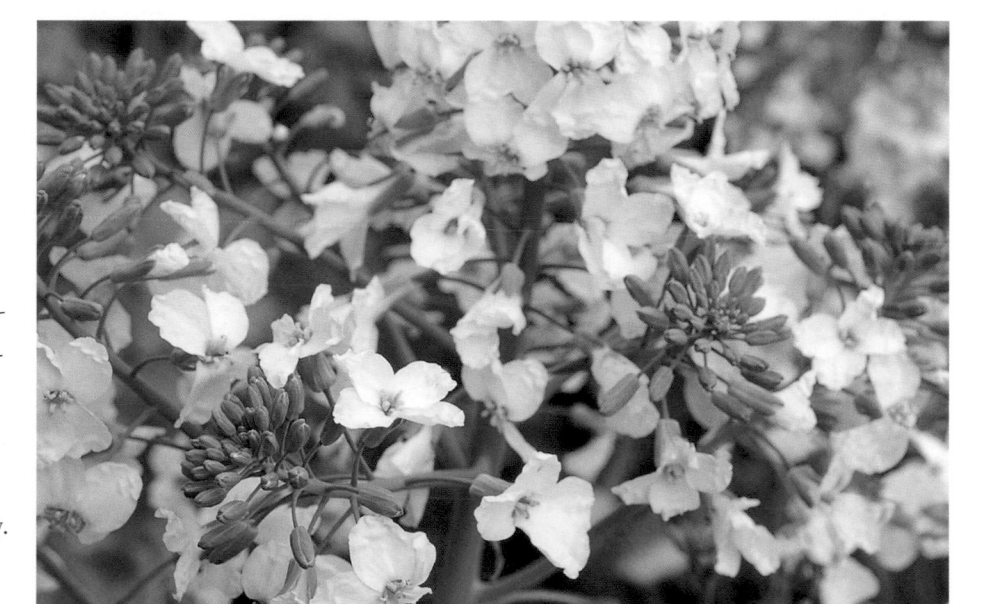

THERE ARE MANY TYPES OF broccoli: the standard heading types, sprouting broccoli, and broccoli raab—all of which produce yellow flowers—and a primitive type with very tiny buds and white flowers, called *sparachetti*, in Italy.

How to grow: Standard broccoli is an annual that prefers cool weather. Plant broccoli in very early spring for summer bearing, or in the summer or fall for winter bearing. Plant seeds, or place transplants in rich soil about two weeks before the last average frost date. All broccolis are heavy feeders that need a consistent supply of water and nutrients. Flea beetles, imported cabbageworm, and cutworms may be problems. Once the primary head is harvested, most broccoli varieties produce many smaller heads—the so-called sprouting broccolis produce side buds more readily than some of the modern heading varieties do.

How to prepare: Broccoli buds open up and produce clusters of yellow or white flowers that have a mild broccoli flavor. Incorporate them into hot pasta with broccoli florets and braised onions. Sprinkle them whole over green salads, grated carrot or cucumber salads, cold red pepper soup, gazpacho, black bean soup, and poached fish. They can also be combined with other flowers in a petal confetti.

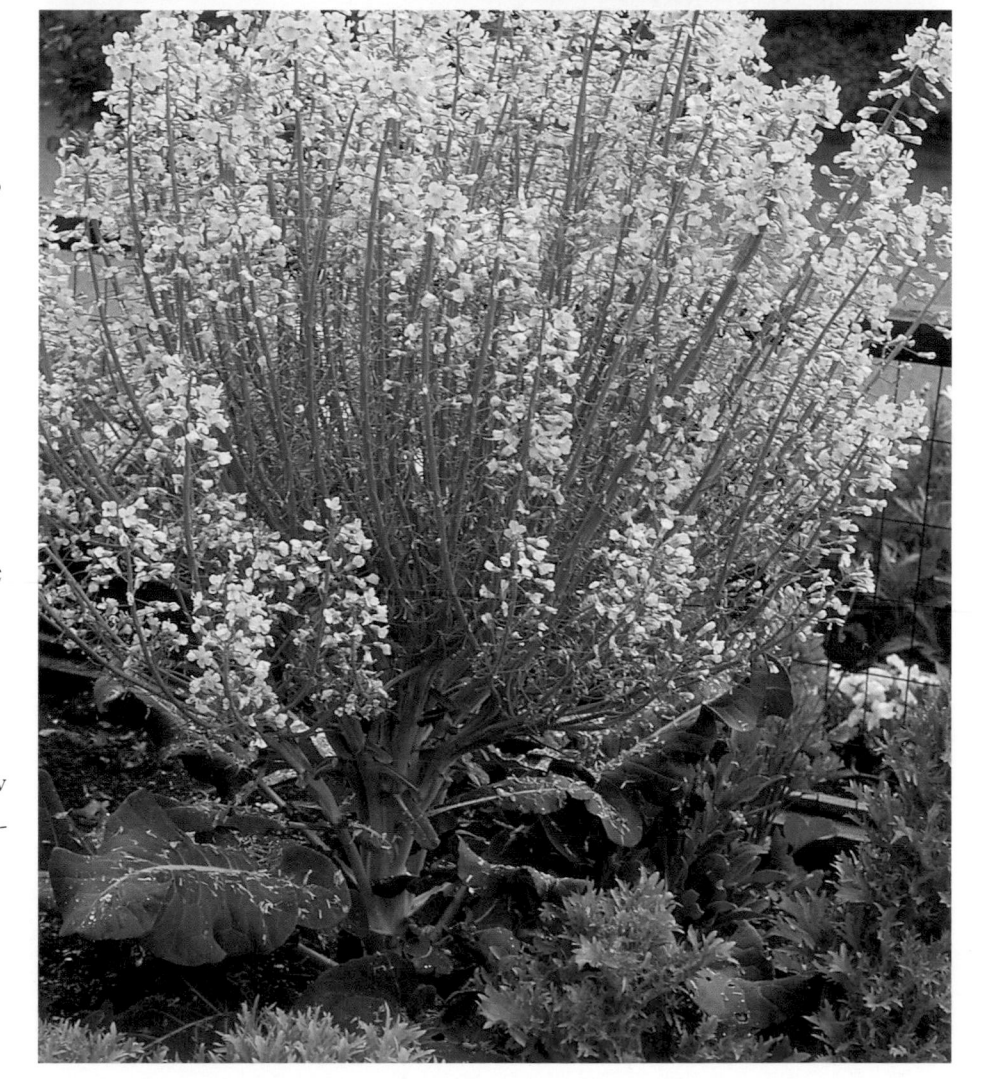

'Sparachetti' broccoli flowers (*top*, seeds are available in Italian grocery stores and offered by Pagano's Seeds); standard broccoli (*bottom*)

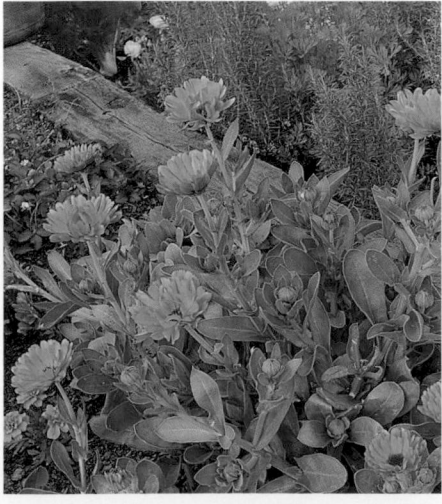

'Pacific Beauty' calendula flower (*top*), 'Bon Bon' calendula (*middle*), 'Pacific Beauty' plants with rosemary (*bottom*)

CALENDULA
Calendula officinalis

CALENDULA, ALSO KNOWN AS pot marigold, was a popular edible flower as far back as ancient Rome, when the peasants used it as a substitute for the very expensive saffron.

How to grow: Calendulas are easily grown cool-season annuals that do best in fairly rich, fast-draining soil in full sun. The orange, apricot, cream, or yellow flowers can be single or double. I think the slightly sticky 2-inch green leaves have a "grassy" aroma. Tall varieties such as 'Pacific Beauty' and 'Kablouna' grow to more than 2 feet tall; dwarf varieties such as 'Bon Bon,' 'Radio,' and 'Fiesta' grow to 1 foot.

In cold-winter areas with a short spring and fall, plant seeds in flats six weeks before setting the plants outside; because calendulas can tolerate light frosts, plant calendulas in the fall in mild-winter areas. Most nurseries carry transplants in both the spring and fall. Space plants about 18 inches apart and water them in well. To keep them healthy, keep the soil evenly moist and watch for slugs and snails. Mildew is a common problem, especially in warm weather. The dwarf varieties seem to be more prone to this disease. 'Pacific Beauty' is one of the older varieties and often reseeds itself in mild climates. Other full-size varieties include the heirloom 'Radio' with its large orange petals and the double-petaled 'Kablouna.' Two dwarf varieties, 'Fiesta' and 'Bon Bon,' have double flowers in a mix of yellow, cream, and orange. Calendulas make great cut flowers as well. For continual blooms, remove the spent flowers.

How to prepare: Calendula petals have a slightly tangy, bitter taste; they are often used more for their color than for their flavor. The varieties 'Pacific Beauty' and 'Radio' are easier to clean than the double varieties. To prepare calendula flowers, remove the petals from the 2- or 3-inch-wide heads and use them whole or chop them before adding them to cooked dishes such as soups, soufflés, rice dishes, muffins and biscuits, and omelets and frittatas. Vinegar infused with calendula petals and either dill or thyme makes a lovely condiment. Mince the petals to incorporate into butters and soft cheeses. To release the oils and color from the petals most effectively, include a little oil in the recipe. Whole petals can be used to garnish salads, soups, frittatas, and rice dishes. Use dried petals all winter long in soups and rice pilaf.

'Kablouna' calendulas with frost on the flowers

CHAMOMILE

Chamaemelum nobile,
Matricaria recutita

THERE ARE TWO KINDS OF chamomile—the perennial type, which is low growing and moderately hardy, and an annual chamomile, which is a lovely short-lived garden flower.

How to grow: The annual chamomile, sometimes called German chamomile, grows to about 18 inches and produces a cloud of small white daisies. It has a sweeter taste and is less medicinal tasting. Many people feel that its flowers make a better tea than those from the perennial chamomile. Start both types from seeds in well-

prepared soil, in full sun. Keep them fairly moist. Perennial chamomile can be grown from transplants from the nursery. It is hardy to USDA Zone 4. Both chamomiles are quite free of most pests and diseases.

How to prepare: Most cooks prefer the flavor of the annual chamomile. The perennial is most often used medicinally. Use the flower heads fresh or dried in herbal teas served either hot or iced. Combine the chamomile flowers with other herbs such as lemon verbena, roselle, and mint to make a more complex tea. Sprinkle the petals over salads, especially ones containing apples—the chamomile brings out their taste.

German chamomile

CHIVES AND SOCIETY GARLIC

Allium spp., and
Tulbaghia violacea

HERB SOPHISTICATES AS WELL AS beginners enjoy chives. The blossoms can be used in just about any dish that calls for onions. A chive relative, society garlic grows in tufts of flat leaves and produces heads of lavender flowers that have a pronounced garlic flavor.

How to grow: There are two types of culinary chives: *A. schoenoprasum,* sometimes called onion chives, has a mild onion flavor, tubular grasslike leaves to 18 inches high, and globe-shaped lavender flowers. *A. tuberosum,* Oriental or garlic chives, is a distant relative and has an onion/garlic flavor, flat leaves to 2 feet tall, and white star-shaped flowers. The common variety of Oriental chives blooms only once a year, producing small flower buds. One type of garlic chives called Chinese leek has been bred for its flower buds, which are favored in China. Its seeds are available from Evergreen Y. H. Enterprises. Both types of chives are perennial plants hardy to USDA Zone 3.

Society garlic is a graceful plant that is used in mild-winter areas in herb gardens and as a low-maintenance, drought- and heat-tolerant ornamental. Hardy to 20°F, the plants have gray-green straplike leaves and produce 2-foot-tall flower stalks. A silver-and-white variegated form is more compact and is slow growing.

Chives and society garlic need at least six hours of sun a day and average

to rich, well-drained, moist soil. They are best planted in the spring; obtain divisions, purchase transplants, or grow them from seeds. Richters Herb Catalogue carries a variety of onion chives. One, 'Profusion,' is bred for its flowers, which remain edible for an extended time because they don't set seeds. (Once mature, the seed capsules produced by most varieties make the flowers feel papery in your mouth.) Plant onion chives and the variegated society garlic in the front of, or as a border to, your herb or flower beds and in the vegetable garden.

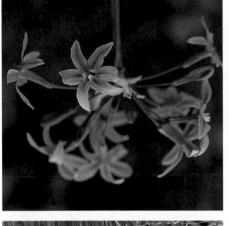

Chives growing along a walk (*top left*), and a detail of chive flower (*left*); Oriental chives (*top*), and a detail of the society garlic flower (*bottom*)

Oriental chives and the standard society garlic, being taller, look best interplanted among other herbs and flowers or in stand-alone beds or in containers.

To keep chives growing well, apply nitrogen fertilizer in the spring or if the leaves yellow. In rainy areas supplemental watering is seldom needed. Pests, except for occasional aphids, and diseases are few and far between.

Common chives bloom in early summer; most Oriental chives bloom in early fall. The Chinese leeks bloom at least twice throughout the spring and summer. Society garlic blooms from late spring to late fall.

Cut back chive plants after they flower, to renew the plant and prevent them from reseeding and becoming a nuisance. Society garlic looks best if the dead flower stalks are removed every month or so. To keep them healthy, divide your plants every three or four years.

How to prepare: Common chive blossoms are among the most versatile edible flowers, tasting as they do of sweet onions. Harvest the flowers just after they open, as the petals of the onion chives are pleasantly crunchy when young, but fibrous when mature. Pull apart all chive florets and sprinkle them as you would the leaves. Use the flowers in salads, sauces, or dips; make chive blossom butter to melt over vegetables; and combine the flowers with sour cream, and cream or goat cheeses. Add chive florets to herbal vinegars. Shower them over a tomato cream soup or vichyssoise, add them to a chicken stir-fry, and use them in stuffed eggs and omelets. Chinese leeks are generally blanched in the garden by cutting them to the ground and covering them to exclude the light for a few weeks—the resulting tender yellow stalks and buds are eaten as a stir-fry vegetable. Society garlic flowers are compatible with most recipes that use garlic or onion. They are popular flowers in California wine country cuisine, where they are commonly added to salads, used as garnishes, and are spectacular folded into a hot pasta dish.

CHRYSANTHEMUMS
Chrysanthemum X morifolium,
Dendranthema X Grandiflora

BLOOMING CHRYSANTHEMUMS are a sign of fall, but few folks think to bring their harvest colors to the table.

How to grow: Chrysanthemums are perennial plants whose flowers come in nearly every color of the rainbow (except blue and a true pink or red) and range in size from 1 to 5 inches across. Buy plants in the spring from a local nursery and plant them in the garden or in containers in good soil, in full sun. To avoid spindly plants, pinch them back frequently until late summer to encourage branching. Water during dry weather. Aphids are an occasional problem.

Garland chrysanthemum (shungiku greens) are grown for their greens in Asia and produce 1-inch yellow flowers with short petals.

Caution: Avoid nursery-grown or florist chrysanthemums because they are usually grown with chemicals that are not allowed on food by the USDA.

Standard chrysanthemums (*top*); 'Garland' or 'shungiku' chrysanthemums (*bottom*)

How to prepare: Chrysanthemum petals have a mild to strong bitter taste, depending on the variety. Use the petals in salads and tea or sprinkle them over clear soups. The varieties with large, open petals are the easiest to work with. Use the petals to garnish stir-fries and one-pot dishes.

Cilantro

CILANTRO

(Fresh coriander)

Coriandrum sativum

THE PUNGENT HERB CILANTRO looks a bit like parsley but tastes very different. Some people strongly dislike the earthy flavor of the leaves and flowers, but others crave it. Known in the Americas as cilantro, or even Chinese parsley, in the Orient this herb is referred to as coriander. Because the plants go to flower so quickly, using the flowers is a way to extend the season.

How to grow: This easily grown annual herb does best in cool weather. It goes to flower readily when the days start to lengthen in the spring and in warm weather. Most gardeners grow cilantro for its leaves; the flowers are just a bonus. Cilantro grown for its leaves is best planted in the fall in all climates. In cold-winter areas the seeds sprout the next spring after the ground thaws, and in mild-winter areas the plants grow lush and tall all over the winter but generally do not bloom until spring. (Cilantro tolerates light frosts.) Gardeners in short-spring areas should start with early plantings; the plants usually go to flower within 60 days.

Plant cilantro seeds ¼ inch deep in rich, light soil and in full sun. Thin them to 6 inches apart. Keep the plants moist to ensure lush growth. Harvest the leaves once the plants are 6 inches tall. Fertilize only if the plants get pale. Cilantro has few pests and diseases. Cilantro flowers, tiny flat sprays of white petals, are produced in profusion in the spring and summer. Not only are they edible, but they are great for attracting beneficial insects to your garden. Harvest them anytime they appear.

How to prepare: Cilantro leaves and flowers are almost always used raw, as the flavor fades quickly when cooked. Use whole flower heads as a garnish for green and savory vegetable salads and on cumin-sprinkled grilled chicken and fancy Southwestern spicy dishes. To incorporate the flowers into a dish, remove the small florets from the stems, which tend to be fairly tough. Chop the florets and add them sparingly to salads, quesadillas, coconut curries, stir-fries, and refried beans or fold them into cooked vegetable dishes and salsa.

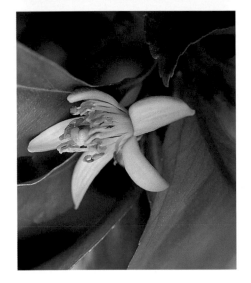

Close-up of a lemon blossom (*top*); orange blossoms (*bottom*)

CITRUS BLOSSOMS

(Lemon and orange)

Citrus limonia and C. sinensis

THE SCENT OF CITRUS BLOS- SOMS is breathtaking; being able to bring it to the table is a bonus.

How to grow: Lemons and oranges are evergreen shrubs or trees that bloom at different times depending on

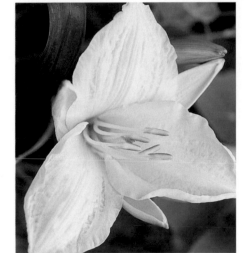

the variety. Obtain plants from local nurseries or by mailorder from Logee's Greenhouses (see Resources, page 103). Plant trees in the spring in rich, well-drained soil or in containers. Keep the plants well watered and fertilize them with citrus fertilizer. Gardeners in USDA Zones 3 through 8 can grow citrus plants in a cool greenhouse in the winter and then move the plants outdoors in the summer. Spider mites and scale are occasional problems.

How to prepare: Many varieties of oranges have a very strong rindlike taste, but others are wonderful in syrups or jams and as a garnish. Taste a few petals before you decide how to use them. Lemon blossoms vary too. Some varieties have a strong rind taste; others, such as 'Meyer,' have a pleasant lemon taste. Use the petals to flavor whipped cream, ice cream, puddings, and lemonade—even vodka. Sprinkle these cream-colored petals on fruit salads and soups and incorporate them into a beurre blanc for fish and chicken. Use them to garnish a pork tenderloin or duck breast served with caramelized onions or over lemon-filled blintzes. If you want to candy whole citrus blossoms, a mixture of confectioner's sugar and egg whites hides the brown tinge of the petals when it dries. Apply this mix lightly and evenly and paint toward the center of the blossom, as the petals come off very easily (see "Candied Flowers," page 72).

DAYLILIES
Hemerocallis spp.

CHEERFUL DAYLILIES PRODUCE flowers that bloom for only one day—hence the name. Asians have enjoyed the blossoms for centuries.

How to grow: Daylilies come in all colors (except pure white and blue), including multicolor and single-color yellow, orange, and bronze; range in length from 2 to 5 inches long, and grow from 18 inches to 3 feet tall. These wonderful plants, particularly some of the older varieties, are hardy perennials that just want to grow. Buy plants from local nurseries and mail-order firms. Although you can use all varieties, the lighter-colored ones tend to be less astringent. Give all daylilies good soil in either light shade or full sun. Fertilize occasionally and keep fairly moist.

How to prepare: The taste of daylily petals ranges from sweet floral to slightly metallic; be sure to taste them before using them in a recipe. The buds have long been used in Chinese stir-fries and Japanese tempura. Called golden needles, the buds are tradition-ally chosen the day before they open for hot and sour soups. The buds taste like a cross between asparagus and green beans. They can also be sautéed or baked. Sliced daylily petals are used in salads and soups; once the stamens and pistils are removed, the whole flower can be stuffed with cheese or bread crumbs and sautéed, or used for a fancy wine-glass presentation of ice cream or sorbet. The sweet varieties make a tasty sorbet.

DILL

Anethum graveolens

DILL IS MOST FAMOUS IN pickles, but the young leaves, florets, and seeds can be used in a variety of dishes.

How to grow: Start these annual plants in the spring from seeds after the weather has warmed up. Plant them in full sun, in well-drained, fertile soil. These ferny plants grow to 3 feet and produce flat sprays of yellow flowers when the plants are a few months old. Keep dill moist throughout the growing season and harvest leaves as soon as the plants get 4 inches tall. Harvest flowers when they appear and use them before the florets start to turn brown.

How to prepare: Break up the flower heads and use them in salads and omelets; sprinkled over vegetable dishes, especially those with spinach, carrots, beets, and potatoes; in fish sauces; and with mild soft cheeses. Use the whole flower heads in jars of cucumber, snap bean, and beet pickles or to add a decorative touch in a bottle of herb-flavored vinegar.

ELDERBERRY FLOWERS

Sambucus canadensis, S. caerulea

THESE EASILY GROWN SHRUBS bloom in late spring with showy, fragrant white flowers.

Caution: Be sure to get the cultivated edible varieties, as some of the wild, red-berried varieties are poisonous.

How to grow: Elderberries are easily grown deciduous shrubs that are available from local nurseries or fruit tree specialists. It's best to plant them in out-of-the-way areas because the berries are messy, and the plants can get quite large, up to 10 feet wide. The plants grow best where the winters are cold. They need full sun, good soil, and severe annual pruning.

How to prepare: The cream-colored elderberry blossoms grow in large clusters. Use only the florets, as all other parts of the plants, including the stems, are poisonous. The most popular recipe for elderberry flowers is to dip the florets in a batter and cook them as fritters. The petals can also be added to jams and jellies. Dried blossoms can be used for either hot or cold tea.

Dill flowers close up (*left*), dill growing with parsley and Johnny-jump-ups (*center*), and flowering elderberry (*right*)

ENGLISH DAISY

Bellis perennis

YOU STILL FIND THE ORIGINAL English daisies growing in lawns in mild-winter areas. The ones sold in nurseries with pink, red, or white double flowers are horticultural varieties that have been selected over the years for larger and fuller flowers.

How to grow: English daisies are technically perennials, but they act more like biennials in mild climates and are treated as annuals in cold climates. Seldom exceeding 6 inches in height and growing from a central cluster, they thrive in full sun, moist soil, and temperate climates, where, if the spent heads are kept trimmed, they bloom again in early fall. In mild-winter areas sow the seeds directly in late summer, or set out plants in late winter. In cold-winter climates start the seeds indoors midwinter and move plants outside after your last expected frost date. English daisies bloom in the spring and early summer and combine well in flower beds with tulips, pansies, and violas—all edible flowers.

How to prepare: The petals of the English daisy have a slightly bitter flavor and are most commonly used as a garnish sprinkled on salads, soups, and steamed vegetables.

English daisies

FENNEL
Foeniculum vulgare

THIS HERB HAS BEAUTIFUL ferny foliage and lovely yellow flowers that closely resemble dill.

How to grow: Though a perennial, fennel is usually grown as you would dill (see above). There are both green and bronze types. Both grow in a similar manner. Cut back the plants in the spring to keep them looking trim. Keep the seed heads removed, as fennel reseeds itself and becomes a weed in many parts of the country. Fennel is a favorite food of the swallowtail butterfly larvae.

How to prepare: Use the florets to garnish dishes made with fennel; over broiled fish, in a remoulade; and chopped and added to potato, tomato, beet, and artichoke dishes.

HONEYSUCKLE
Lonicera japonica

JAPANESE HONEYSUCKLE was probably one of the few flowers we grew up eating. Remember when we would pull the flowers off the vine and suck the sweet juice from the bottom of the flower?

Caution: Only the Japanese species of honeysuckle is documented as being edible.

How to grow: No one should be encouraged to plant Japanese honeysuckle, because this huge vine has become an invasive pest in many parts of the country. Instead, I suggest that you seek out a plant and ask the owner if you may harvest some flowers. The yellow to buff flowers bloom in late spring and sporadically throughout the summer.

How to prepare: The flavor of honeysuckle is but a distillation of its perfume, plus a little sweetness. Infuse the flowers by themselves or in combination with strawberries to make a sorbet, or steep them to make a hot tea. Use the whole flowers to garnish a fruit salad.

LAVENDER

(English or French)

Lavandula angustifolia (officinalis)

THE SCENT OF LAVENDER IS among the most treasured in the Western world. Few folks think of feasting on the flowers, and thus they miss the opportunity to enjoy lavender to a fuller extent.

How to grow: Lavender plants grow to 3 feet and are hardy to USDA Zone 5. The foliage of most lavenders is gray, and the flowers lavender. Start lavender from cuttings or transplants and plant it in full sun. One variety, 'Lady,' starts readily from seeds and, unlike most lavenders, blooms the first year. Watering is usually needed only in arid climates and when the plant is grown in containers, and then only when the soil is fairly dry. Shear back the plants after they bloom. Like most Mediterranean herbs, lavender does poorly in heavy or poorly drained soil and succumbs to root rot readily. In hot weather, lavender occasionally becomes infested with spider mites.

Lavender flowers can be used fresh or dried. When using them fresh, cut the flower stalks and remove the tiny flowers by hand. To harvest them for drying, cut the flower stalks just as they start to bloom and hang them upside down in a warm dark place. Remove the tiny dry flowers as you need them or take them off the stems and store them in a tightly covered container.

How to prepare: With the strong lemon-perfume taste of the petals of its 2-inch flower heads, lavender is one of the most useful culinary flowers. Leaves and flower heads can be steeped for making jellies, sorbets, caramel custard, and ice cream. Use the flowers to flavor a simple syrup that can be drizzled over poached pears or an almond tart. Lavender can be used in lemonade and vinegars and to flavor sugar, which can then be used for sweetening teas or to make short-bread or sugar cookies. (See recipe, page 90.) Traditionally lavender buds are one of the many flavorings of herbes de Provence.

'Dwarf' English lavender

'Munstead' lavender

LILACS
Syringa vulgaris

LILACS MARK MANY A PROPERTY line in this country, and most of us cherish the thought of their lovely perfume.

How to grow: Lilacs are large deciduous shrubs that bloom with lavender or white flowers in the spring in cold-winter areas. Lilacs grow poorly in warm-winter areas. Buy plants from a nursery or order special varieties from mail-order firms. If possible, taste the variety before planting it since not all lilacs have a pleasant floral taste. Plant lilacs in neutral, fast-draining soil in a sunny location. Prune the lilac after it blooms by removing the spent flowers and shaping the shrub to keep it blooming and looking trim. To renew the plant, every few years cut some of the oldest stems almost to the ground and shorten some of the longest, lanky growth back to a strong horizontal branch. Apply a mulch of rotted manure every two years in the fall. Stem borers, leaf miners, and mildew are common problems.

How to prepare: Pick the flower heads soon after they open. Remove the individual florets and add them to soft cheeses or frozen yogurt or use them to garnish all sorts of sweet dishes, such as a plate of cookies, cakes, and scones.

Marigold, 'Lemon Gem'

Lilac

MARIGOLDS
Tagetes

SOME MARIGOLD FLOWERS can be rather smelly and unappetizing, but a few varieties have a pleasant citrus flavor.

How to grow: Marigolds are summer annuals that are easily grown when given fast-draining, fairly rich soil and full sun. I find 'Lemon Gem' and 'Tangerine Gem' to be the tastiest varieties. These flavorful marigolds produce clouds of ½-inch flowers. There are also some light-colored varieties; 'French Vanilla' and 'Aurora Light Yellow' have a mild flavor, and the petals are useful as a garnish and in a petal confetti. Because these varieties are often not sold in local nurseries, you usually have to order seeds and start the plants yourself. Start seeds inside in the spring and transplant them after any threat of frost is over, placing them about 1 foot apart. Keep the plants fairly moist and mulch to keep them healthy. The plants will produce flowers until the fall. Young marigolds are a delicacy to slugs and snails, leaf miners sometimes tunnel through the foliage, and spider mites are sometimes a problem in hot weather.

How to prepare: Use marigold flowers sparingly in salads and as garnishes. Use the more flavorful 'Gem' varieties in deviled eggs, in marigold butter, sprinkled over broccoli and other assertive vegetables.

MUSTARD
(India Mustard)
JAPANESE RED MUSTARD, SPINACH MUSTARD
Brassica juncea, B. spp.

A NUMBER OF GREENS referred to as mustards produce flowers that are edible and have a slight mustard taste.

How to grow: Mustards are cool-season crops grown like broccoli (see above). Plant seeds in early spring in full sun, in rich, fertile loam. Thin to 1 foot apart. All mustards are members of the cabbage family and may occasionally be plagued by the same pests. The leaves may be harvested as needed before the plant is left to flower.

How to prepare: Mustard flowers add a little bite to a mixed salad. Use them sparingly in salads or sprinkle them on cream soups, in butters, and in dishes where broccoli flowers would be appropriate. Combine them in a salad dressed with a cider vinaigrette or use them in a remoulade. To bring out their flavor, add a little prepared mustard to the salad dressing.

Mustard field in Germany (*above*) and mustard flower (*right*)

NASTURTIUMS

Tropaeolum majus

CHEERY AND PUNGENT, nasturtiums are among my favorite edible flowers. In fact, I've grown whole gardens filled with just nasturtiums.

How to grow: There are almost a dozen varieties of nasturtium on the market, but local nurseries usually carry only a few. Consider starting your own, as they grow best from seeds started directly in the garden. If you've never started flowers from seeds, nasturtiums are a great way to start, even for children. The select varieties include 'Alaska', with green-and-white foliage and flowers of yellow, cream, maroon, and orange; 'Empress of India', with deep red and orange flowers and dark blue green leaves; 'Strawberries and Cream', compact plants with green leaves, cream flowers, and a red throat; and 'Whirlybird', with

green leaves and double flowers of cream, deep red, apricot, and yellow that have no spur at the back of the flower. These are all dwarf varieties that grow to about 1 foot high. There is also a large climbing mix that sprawls to 10 feet; it is sold as "climbing nasturtium" and comes in a mix of colors.

About the date of your last expected frost in the spring, plant seeds ½ inch

A section of my nasturtium garden (*top left*), 'Strawberries and Cream' nasturtiums (*top right*), 'Empress of India' nasturtiums (*bottom*)

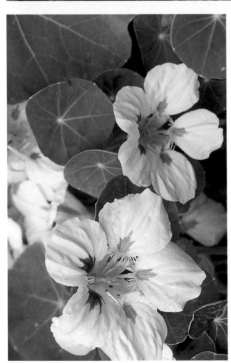

deep in lean to average soil with good drainage. In cool-weather areas plant them in full sun, but provide some afternoon shade in hot climates. Keep the seed bed moist. Make sure the plants don't dry out and watch for

A mix of nasturtium varieties (*top*); 'Whirlybird' nasturtium (*bottom*)

occasional aphids. Nasturtiums have a few quirks: they produce lots of flowers in lean soil and few in rich soil, and they reseed themselves heavily under favorable conditions.

How to prepare: The flowers, leaves, and seed pods of nasturtiums are all edible. The tangy flavor is mustardlike, with an added perfume and sweetness. Harvest the flowers just as they open. I prefer to use small leaves whole and the flowers with their petals removed, but occasionally I serve the flowers whole. They're entirely edible, just a little large. Both the leaves and the flowers are great minced and incorporated into butters and soft cheeses and used to flavor oils, dressings and vinegars, and cucumber sandwiches. The petals can be sprinkled over a green salad and used as a garnish for salads and buffet platters. Stuff whole flowers with flavored soft cheeses or guacamole. It is easier to eat the stuffed blossom on a piece of melba toast or a slice of cucumber or jicama, especially at a buffet table. To temper nasturtiums' bite, add honey or fruit juice to a dressing. The immature seed heads can be pickled and used as you would capers in salads and on pizza.

nasturtiums

51

PEAS
Pisum sativum

PEA FLOWERS ARE SCULPTURAL and taste like the freshest of peas.

Caution: Do not confuse edible pea blossoms with sweet peas, which are poisonous.

How to grow: Peas are cool-season annuals that grow on either bushy plants or tall vines. All edible peas have tasty edible blossoms. Most varieties have white flowers, but a few edible pea varieties produce purple flowers, including 'Dwarf Gray Sugar.' Start peas as soon as the soil can be worked in the spring in rich, fast-draining soil in a sunny part of the garden. Plant the seeds ½ inch deep, 2 inches apart. Give the vining peas a trellis at planting time. Thin the plants to 6 inches apart and keep them moist at all times. Pea plants are prone to a number of diseases, and the seedlings are attacked by slugs, snails, and birds. Harvest some of the flowers as they appear, but don't take too many, or you will cut down on your pea production.

How to prepare: The flowers of some varieties have a "grassy" flavor; others have a mild, sweet, floral taste. Sprinkle them over a lobster bisque for a special garnish. Use them in a mixed or baby greens salad or as a garnish, or candy them to make some extremely pretty candied flowers great for salmon canapés or even a wedding cake.

PINEAPPLE GUAVA
Feijoa sellowiana

THE SUCCULENT PETALS OF pineapple guavas growing in my yard have won many an edible flower convert.

How to grow: Pineapple guava is a evergreen shrub that is native to South America and is hardy to about 20°F. In colder climates the plants can be grown in large containers outside in the summer, to be brought in to a cool greenhouse in the winter. Plant these guavas in rich, well-drained soil, in full sun or light shade and water them moderately. They bloom in late spring, bearing flowers with big tufts of red stamens and five fleshy white petals. The variety that is generally available is 'Pineapple Gem.' Squirrels and some birds feast on the petals, so I cover a few branches with bird netting. Flowers left to develop produce juicy, tangy gray green fruit about 2 inches long in midsummer.

How to prepare: The flowers of the pineapple guava have a sweet and tropical-guava flavor. The only part of the flower that is eaten, the petals are delicious used as a garnish to a tropical fruit salad or cold drinks, eaten with avocados, and added to tropical jellies and fruit salsas.

'Dwarf Gray Sugar' pea blossoms (*top*), 'Tall Telephone' blossoms (*middle*), a pineapple guava flower (*bottom*)

Dianthus 'Horatio' (*top*), Cottage pinks (*middle*); radish flowers (*bottom*) are not only tasty, they attract beneficial insects such as this syphid fly

PINKS

Dianthus spp.

PINKS WERE POPULAR IN OUR grandmother's day and often lined a front walk or flower bed.

How to grow: Though called pinks, dianthus has pink, rose, white, or red flowers. Pinks are easily grown perennials that are at home in a rock garden or flower border. They are hardy, and some varieties bloom most of the summer. They grow best in full sun, in rich, well-drained soil. Start them from seeds or divisions, or buy plants from the nursery. The best-tasting ones are the small, fragrant clove pinks, D. *caryophyllus*, or cottage pinks, D. *plumarius*.

How to prepare: Pinks have a pleasant spicy, floral, clovelike taste. The 1- to 2-inch blossoms can be steeped in wine; made into syrup, sorbets, or custard; chopped and mixed into butter; and used to garnish cakes, salads, soups, and the punch bowl. Taste your flowers first: sometimes the white base of the petals is bitter. If so, remove it.

RADISHES

Raphanus sativus

RADISH FLOWERS COME in pink, lavender, and white. They are produced when the plants are allowed to bolt but before they go to seed, a frequent occurrence since the plants are so short-lived.

How to grow: Obviously, the point of growing radishes is to produce the roots; the flowers are just a bonus. Sow seeds directly in the garden after the last frost, or sow them in early fall. Radishes prefer cool weather. Plant seeds ½ inch deep, and thin to 2 inches apart. The soil should be light and well drained. Keep the young radishes constantly moist. Most varieties are ready in a month and bloom a few weeks later. In some areas of the country radishes are bothered by root maggots. Flea beetles can also be a considerable problem.

How to prepare: Harvest the small flower spikes and put them in water until you are ready to serve them. Remove the individual flowers from the stems and sprinkle them over a salad or over cooked vegetables. Radish flowers can be used in the same way as broccoli and mustard flowers (see above). In addition, use them in a salad of julienned daikon to enhance the flavor and give color.

REDBUD

(Judas Tree)

Cercis canadensis,
Cercis siliquastrum

REDBUDS ARE LOVELY SMALL trees with spectacular magenta flowers in the spring and rounded, gray green leaves throughout the summer.

How to grow: Redbuds bloom in early spring. Plant them in full sun or partial shade, in sandy loam. They grow well under larger trees in a woodland garden and in cold climates, as they need some winter chill to flower. Redbuds are available profusely from local nurseries. Varieties to look for include 'Flame,' which has double pink flowers; 'Rubye Atkinson,' with its pure pink flowers; and 'Silver Cloud,' which has marbled foliage. Harvest the flower spikes and break off the small flowers before serving.

How to prepare: Redbud flowers can be picked either as buds or when in full flower. They have long been popular in Italy. Buds can be pickled in vinegar, like capers. Make the flower clusters into fritters and fry them in batter. They also add a pleasant crunch to salads or can be used as a garnish for cooked vegetables. The flavor is a cross between green beans and a tart apple.

ROSEMARY

Rosmarinus officinalis

ROSEMARY IS A PUNGENT, resinous herb native to the Mediterranean.

How to grow: A tender perennial, rosemary needs full sun and fast-draining soil. In USDA Zones 8 and colder, it is usually grown as an annual or planted in containers and brought inside for the winter. Most varieties produce a profusion of light blue flowers in the spring, but other colors include light blue, deep blue, lavender, pink, and white.

The standard culinary rosemary has light blue flowers, as does 'Arp,' which is reputed to be the hardiest variety, to 10°F; 'Irene' and 'Tuscan Blue' have dark blue flowers; and 'Majorca Pink' has pink ones. You can purchase the unusual varieties from specialty herb nurseries.

Gardeners everywhere have trouble with root rot if the drainage is poor, and spider mites are occasionally a problem in hot weather or when rosemary is grown inside. Gardeners in the South may have problems with nematodes. Harvest the flowering stems or individual flowers.

How to prepare: The small and slightly resinous flowers make a lovely confetti to sprinkle over salads and vegetable dishes. Rosemary flowers are compatible with many dishes containing pork, duck, and lamb and can be sprinkled over salmon, scallops, and swordfish; included in a pilaf; added to a butter sauce to dress grilled eggplants and mushrooms; or used on top of roasted potatoes. The flowers can also be added to herb vinegars. Whole flowering stems can be used to garnish a buffet platter.

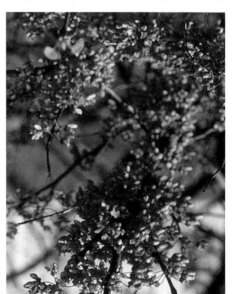

Redbud *(left)* and Rosemary 'Tuscan Blue' *(right)*

ROSES

Rosa spp.

ROSE FLOWERS HAVE BEEN USED in cooking since ancient times in both Europe and Asia.

How to grow: Rose flowers come in a range of colors, from red through yellow. All are edible, but the heirlooms such as *Rosa gallica*, the gallicas; *R. moschata*, the musk roses; *R. centifolia*, the centifolia or cabbage roses; and *R. damascena*, the damask roses, are usually the most hardy, disease resistant, and fragrant; thus they are usually the most flavorful. Most of these heirloom roses grow to be very large plants and, with few exceptions, bloom only in the spring.

Other roses you might choose from include 'Cécile Brünner,' a small, pink sweetheart rose; 'Zéphirine Drouhin,' a very fragrant, bright pink rose; 'Austrian Copper,' a deep-orange single rose; 'Eglantine,' a small, deep pink rose that smells like apples; 'Belinda,' a small, deep pink rose particularly good for candying whole; *Rugosa alba*, a hardy, lovely, fragrant white single flower that's one of the tastiest and best for sorbet. All are quite disease resistant and need little spraying in most climates. Again, most bloom only once in the spring, though a few give a sparse bloom in late summer. Other roses that have little fragrance but are lovely for garnishing include 'The

Roses, clockwise from top: 'Perfect Moment,' an old moss rose, 'Iceberg,' Luther Burbank's rose, the deep orange 'Austrian Copper,' and 'Graham Thomas.'

Fairy,' 'Carefree Delight,' and 'Jeanne Lajoie.' Varieties I've enjoyed that take more care but are tasty and beautiful and bloom all summer are 'Graham Thomas' and 'Perfect Moment.'

Cathy Barash, edible flower maven, who grows roses extensively in USDA Zone 5, likes to recommend 'Tiffany,' 'Mr. Lincoln,' 'Double Delight,' 'Mirandy,' and 'Pink Flower Carpet' (which is not fragrant but has a pleasant taste) as fairly hardy if given winter protection, good for the kitchen, and resistant to diseases in the New York area. They all bloom throughout the summer.

Rosebushes are best planted bare root in early spring. Appendices A and B (pages 92–102) give basic information on planting and maintaining

the "easy care" old roses and some of the modern landscape roses. If you choose some of the hybrid tea and floribunda roses, chances are they will need much extra care—fertilizing and substantial disease and pest controls—so you will need to consult some books on roses (see the Bibliography, page 104) to keep them growing well.

Caution: Never eat florist-grown roses, as they usually contain toxic chemicals.

How to prepare: Most rose varieties have a strong floral taste. Some of the dark red varieties can be too strong and metallic tasting. With most roses, you need to remove the white part at the base of the petal, as it is bitter.

Individual petals of large varieties and the whole small-flowered roses can be candied and used as a garnish on desserts. Use fragrant rose petals to make jellies, rose water, and vinegars. They can be infused to make flavored honey, butters, and simple and fruit syrups; sprinkled over salads; placed under a sorbet to create a graceful presentation; and used in many ways as a garnish. To make rose sugar, mince 2 cups of fragrant petals and pound them together with a mortar and pestle with 1 cup of granulated sugar. Let the mixture sit for a week, strain out the petals, and store the sugar in an airtight container.

'The Fairy' (left) and 'Pink Flower Carpet' and 'Red Meidiland' roses

SAFFLOWER

Carthamus tinctorius

SAFFLOWERS ARE TALL, STIFF plants with 1-inch thistlelike flowers.

How to grow: Safflower is a tender annual that grows to 3 feet tall. It prefers light, dry, well-drained soil. Plant seeds every 6 inches, about ½ inch deep, after any danger of frost is past. Thin the seedlings to 2 feet apart. Safflower needs full sun. Safflower blooms in midsummer with thistle-shaped flowerheads that turn from deep yellow to deep red as they mature. They have few pest and disease problems.

How to prepare: Safflower petals taste slightly bitter. Remove the petals from the tops of the flowers and use them fresh or dried. In either form the petals give cooked foods a lovely yellow color. Substitute safflower for calendula petals in recipes such as poor man's rice, or sprinkle them over a carrot salad or sliced jicama.

Scarlet runner beans (*top left*), 'Scarlet Bees' runner beans (*top right*), safflower (*above*)

RUNNER BEANS

Phaseolus coccineus

RUNNER BEANS ARE DRAMATIC vines that are covered most of the summer with spikes of small red flowers.

How to grow: Runner beans are grown for their dramatic, long string beans, which are eaten fresh or allowed to dry and then stored for later use. The flowers are just a bonus. These beans grow best in cool-summer areas, and most varieties have large vines with flowers of red orange, white, or, in the case of 'Painted Lady', salmon and white. A dwarf variety, 'Scarlet Bees,' grows to 2 feet and has red flowers. Grow runner beans as you would most snap beans—in good soil, in full sun. Plant the seeds 1 inch deep, 3 inches apart. Thin them to 6 inches apart. Keep the plants fairly moist and protect the seedlings from slugs, snails, and bean beetles. The plants flower within a few months and produce beans if the weather stays in the low 80s. When temperatures get high, the plants usually produce some flowers but no beans.

How to prepare: Runner bean flowers have a sweet, bean/pea taste and a slightly crunchy texture. Use them to top soups, especially bean soups; in cream cheese appetizer sandwiches; in green and bean salads; and as a garnish for steamed snap beans and white bean puree.

Common purple sage (*top*) and the less common white variation (*bottom*)

SAFFRON

Crocus sativus

PROBABLY ONE OF THE world's most expensive flavorings, the spice consists of the dried, pulverized stig-mas of a fall-blooming crocus.

How to grow: Plant the corms of these crocuses in late summer. They are available from a few specialty seed companies and nurseries. Hardy to USDA Zone 6, these plants prefer rich, well-drained soil with some afternoon shade. Plant these pretty, mauve to purple crocuses in large quantities if you wish to harvest them for the saf-fron, since a suitable harvest requires many plants. Divide and replant every two years.

Caution: Do not confuse saffron crocus with the autumn crocus, *Colchicum*, which is poisonous.

How to prepare: Remove the orange stigmas with tweezers, dry them for a few days, and store them in a covered jar in a warm, dry place. Grind and use them in rice dishes, including pilaf and paella; with seafoods; and in East Indian dishes. Saffron also adds a gorgeous golden color to bundt cakes and the famous French fish soup bouillabaisse.

SAGE

Salvia officinalis, S. elegans

SAGE FLOWERS ARE spectacular spikes of purple or red flowers; they taste like the leaves, only a little sweeter. Not all culinary sages bloom, so look for specific varieties that have flowers.

How to grow: Most culinary sages are perennials that are grown from cuttings. Common sage is hardy to USDA Zone 4 if given protection in the coldest regions. Pineapple sages are hardy only to USDA Zone 7. Most sages do poorly in hot, humid climates and are treated as annuals in the Deep South. Plant sage in average soil with extremely good drainage and in full sun. In hot weather, and on house-grown sages, spider mites are occasion-ally a problem. For the best flower selection, plant the standard culinary sage, with its gray leaves and spikes of purple or white flowers, in the spring, and pineapple sage, in either its full size or dwarf version with its green leaves and red flower spikes, in the fall. To keep these plants looking neat, trim them back once heavily in the spring and, if leggy, again in the summer. Harvest whole flowering spikes or individual florets.

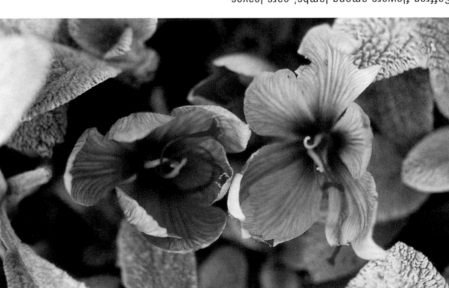

Saffron flowers among lambs' ears leaves

How to prepare: The flower spikes of common sage are great dipped in a tempura batter and deep-fried. Use individual florets to garnish saltimbocca, carpaccio, roast venison, white bean or tomato cream soup, and frittatas. Sprinkle them over a green tossed salad, steamed mussels, or a fennel and orange salad. Add them to a wild mushroom risotto, mince the blossoms and incorporate them into a cheddar or cream cheese spread, or use them in sweet butter to melt over pork or grilled mushrooms. The red spikes of pineapple sage flowers have a distinctive pineapple taste; the individual florets can be used in teas and cold drinks and in tropical fruit salads, jams, jellies, and salsas.

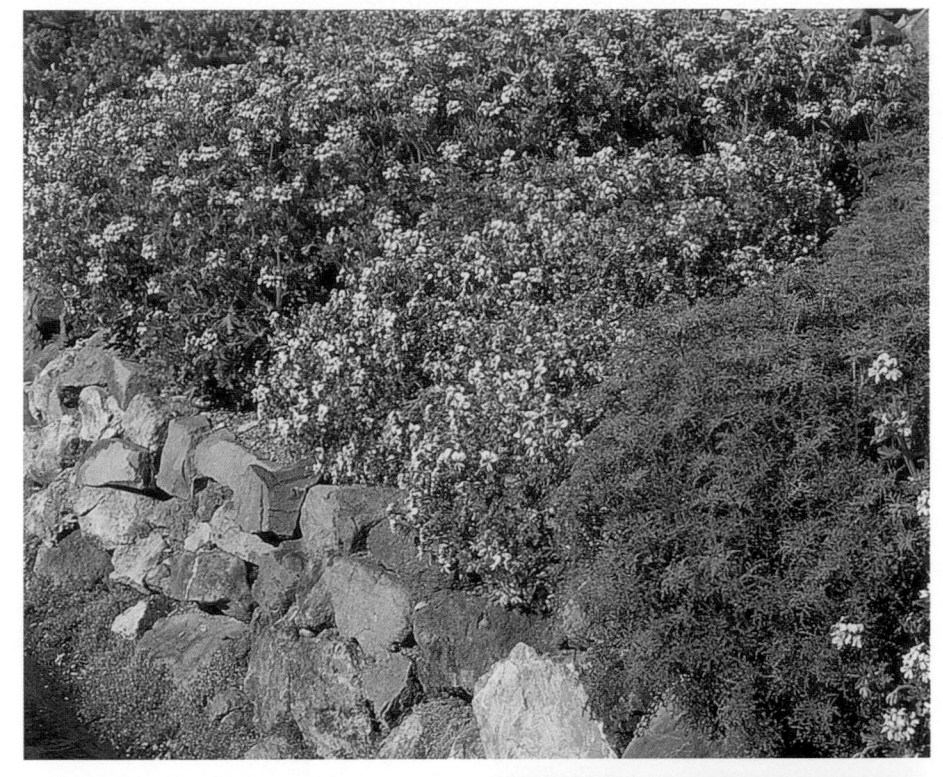

A collection of scented geraniums at the Berkeley Botanical Garden (*above*) and lemon-scented geranium (*right*)

SCENTED GERANIUMS

Pelargonium spp.

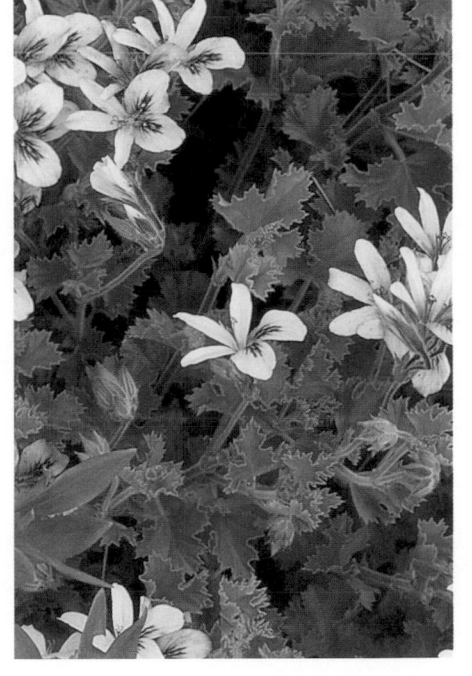

SCENTED GERANIUMS HAVE small edible flowers that are generally pink to rose.

How to grow: The many names of scented geraniums belie their taste. Lemon, mint, chocolate, nutmeg, and rose geraniums produce edible flowers. Only the rose- and lemon-scented ones are worth using in the kitchen, however.

Set out plants from the nursery after the weather warms up, or start them from cuttings earlier in the spring. In climates where winter temperatures stay above 30°F, they can be grown outside year-round. Gardeners in cold climates grow them in containers and bring them inside for the winter. The plants can grow to 3 feet across in mild climates and benefit from annual pruning to keep them neat looking. Plant scented geraniums in full sun or light shade, in well-drained soil. Fertilize and water only occasionally. Harvest individual small flower clusters off the plant and separate them before serving them.

How to prepare: Use the small flowers of rose and lemon geraniums to flavor ice creams and custards or to garnish a fruit salad. Add them to crème fraîche served over strawberries or peaches. Flavor apple jelly with them, and use the jelly between layers of pound cake or as a glaze on a fruit tart. Florets can also be put into a sugar canister to flavor sugar for use in pound cake, sugar cookies, and tea. My greatest success at candying edible flowers has been with scented geraniums; they keep their color and are very flavorful.

SQUASH BLOSSOMS

Cucurbita spp.

ALL SQUASH AND PUMPKINS produce large yellow blossoms that are edible. These flowers have a long history as a delicacy reaching back to the early Native American tribes.

How to grow: All squash are warm-weather crops that grow well in a vegetable garden. Zucchini squash produces the most, and largest, blossoms. Try in particular the varieties 'Clarimore' and 'Gold Rush.' Plant squash seeds 1 inch deep in the spring after any threat of frost has passed. Have the soil filled with well-rotted manure. All squash need full sun. The bush types spread to 3 feet; the large winter squash and pumpkins spread to 12 feet. Keep the soil moist and fertilize midseason with fish meal or emulsion. Where cucumber beetles and squash vine borers are a problem, cover the plants with floating row covers until the blossoms appear.

Try to gather the blossoms in the early morning before they close, and put their bases or stems in water in the refrigerator until you need them. The female flowers have an immature little squash at the base where they meet the stem; the male flowers end at the stem. Most gardeners gather only male blossoms, making sure to leave a few to pollinate the females. If you need to harvest all the male flowers, you can hand-pollinate the remaining females. With a cotton swab or small paint brush, gently rub the anthers on a male flower to obtain pollen. One by one, transfer the pollen to the centers of the female flowers. To slow down summer squash production, to thin a winter squash harvest, or when you are cooking the blossoms as baby squash, harvest females too.

How to prepare: Squash blossoms have a slightly sweet nectar taste. Wash and gently dry the flowers. (Watch out for bees if you are using closed blossoms; the bees sometimes get trapped inside and, contrary to reason, are not happy when you free them!) If you're using the blossoms for fritters or stuffing, keep the stems on. Stuff them with cheeses, bread crumbs, couscous, or meat mixtures and bake or deep-fry them. Don't worry about the sharp prickles—they will wilt during cooking. Otherwise, remove stems, stamens, and stigmas. Some cooks string the blossoms like celery, removing the veins that run down the outside of the flower. Thinly slice the blossoms and use them in cream soups, soufflés, frittatas, omelets, scrambled eggs, burritos; over pasta; and sprinkled on salads accompanied by a pumpkin seed oil vinaigrette.

A basket of squash blossoms (*top*); 'Gold Rush' zucchini blossoms (*bottom*); notice the baby squash at the back of the female flowers

STRAWBERRIES
Fragaria X ananassa

WE GROW STRAWBERRIES for their luscious fruits, but the white single flowers are also edible.

How to grow: Grow strawberries in a vegetable garden in full sun in rich organic soil that is fairly moist. They are hardy to USDA Zone 4. Runners are available from the nursery in the spring. Choose locally adapted, day-neutral or ever-bearing varieties, as they produce for most of the summer. 'Pink Panda' produces lots of pink flowers and few fruits. Plant 1 foot apart. Mulch strawberry plants well and fertilize mid-season with fish emulsion. Harvest occasional flowers and fruits as they appear. Slugs attack both flowers and fruits. During hot weather strawberries are prone to spider mites, and the plants will rot if the drainage is poor.

How to prepare: Sprinkle strawberry petals over salads and candy them whole to use as a garnish for all sorts of deserts.

THYME
Thymus spp.

THYME IS A FRAGRANT HERB from the Mediterranean that produces clouds of small edible flowers.

How to grow: Thyme is hardy to USDA Zone 5, though it needs a protective mulch in the coldest zones. These spreading perennials vary from 4 to 12 inches high and are gray green, dark green, or golden. French thyme, *T. vulgaris*, is the most commonly used culinary thyme and has lavender flowers. Other choice varieties are lemon thyme, *T. citriodorus*, which has a rich lemon taste and pink flowers; and caraway thyme, *T. herba-barona*, with a caraway taste and pink flowers. All thymes need full sun and fast-draining soil. In the spring cut back the foliage by about a third so the plant stays lush. Most gardeners start plants with transplants. Thymes are quite pest and disease resistant.

How to prepare: The tiny pink or lavender flowers are borne on sprigs that are great for garnishing plates and platters. The small flowers can be removed from the stems and sprinkled over soups, salads, sauces, braised rabbit, grilled or poached fish, grilled duck breast, asparagus, and caramelized sweet onions, or they can be incorporated into soft cheeses and butters.

'Lime,' 'French,' 'Wooly' thyme and dianthus

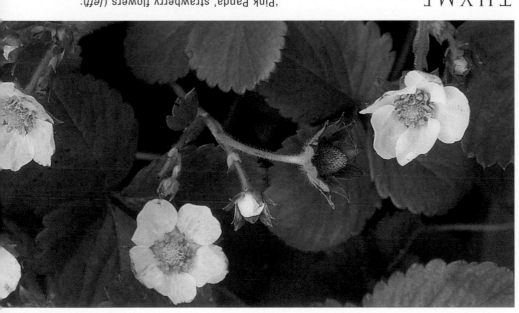

'Pink Panda' strawberry flowers (left); 'Sequoia' strawberry flowers (right)

TULIPS

Tulipa spp.

TULIPS ARE BELOVED HARBINGERS of spring. The flowers can be red, yellow, orange, magenta, pink, lavender, or white, and fluted or smooth.

How to grow: Purchase bulbs at your local nursery. Tulips are hardy plants grown from bulbs set out in fall. Before planting, prepare the bed well and add bonemeal. In large drifts or even in containers, plant the bulbs two and a half times as deep as they are wide. Make the beds in a sunny area in well-draining soil. If rodents are a problem, plant the bulbs in wire baskets and cover the emerging spring shoots with netting.

Caution: A few people are allergic to tulips, so all new diners should proceed with caution. Look for numb hands or an upset stomach.

How to prepare: Tulip petals have a sweet, pealike flavor and a tender, crisp texture. Use them in salads or tea sandwiches. Try arranging the petals on a platter around your favorite savory dip. Or better yet, stuff whole flowers with shrimp or chicken salad for a show-stopper. Carefully remove the pollen and stigmas from the base of the flowers before stuffing them.

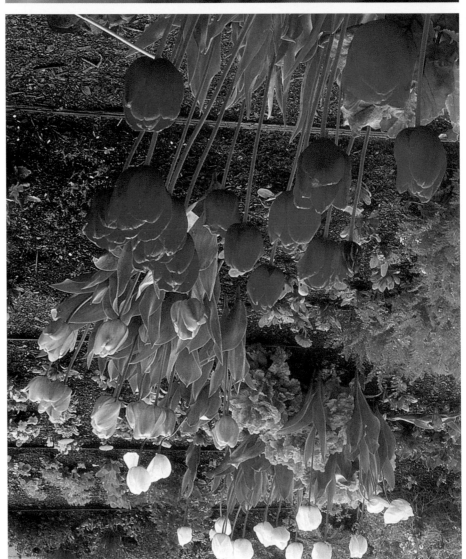

'Balalaika' red, 'Deluxe Goldtech' orange and yellow, 'Jewel of Spring' tulips (*top*); 'Big Chief' tulips (*bottom*)

A mix of 'Universal' pansies (above); Johnny-jump-ups (bottom)

vinegar, the purple flowers turn the mixture lavender.

they can be candied. When infused in a made into a flavorful simple syrup or garnishes, and in salads. They can be beautiful for decorating desserts, as very slight lettucelike taste. They are

How to prepare: The petals have a

themselves in your garden.

Johnny-jump-ups will generally reseed ous rots that attack in humid weather. which eat the emerging buds, and vari- slugs, snails, earwigs, and sowbugs, available. The most notable pests are violas are the varieties most readily 'Universal' pansy and 'Crystal Bowl' old flower heads every few weeks. The keep the flowers coming, remove the every six weeks with fish emulsion. To They can take light frost. Fertilize in moist, rich soil, in partial shade. weather. Plant seeds or bedding plants annual flowers that grow best in cool pending on the variety. They are all about ¼ inch to 3 inches across, de- flowers come in various colors and are

How to grow: These viola-type

mate zones during the cool season. and pansies appear in almost all cli-

THE FRIENDLY FACES OF VIOLAS

Viola cornuta, V. wittrockiana, and V. tricolor

VIOLAS, PANSIES, AND JOHNNY- JUMP-UPS

VIOLETS

Viola odorata

CANDIED VIOLETS HAVE BEEN a treat for centuries and are still available in gourmet shops today.

How to grow: These hardy perennials grow well in a shady, moist corner of the garden in rich soil. The single, so-called wild species of violets grows so readily that it can become a nuisance. You can also obtain many selected cultivars that come in purple, pink, or white. As a rule, these varieties are much less vigorous, and some have no fragrance. Buy the common violets and an occasional named variety at your local nursery, and, if possible, buy them in bloom to ensure they are fragrant. You can probably get divisions of the common violet from a gardening friend. Spider mites can sometimes be a problem in dry climates.

How to prepare: Violets have a strong, sweet, very floral taste. They're great for candying or using plain in desserts, salads, garnishes, and tea sandwiches. Freeze them in ice cubes and float them in a punch bowl. Use violets to scent a sugar bowl, flavor a custard, or color and flavor a vinegar.

Orange 'Crystal Bowl' violas with the edible flowers of mâche (*top*); harvest of pansies and violas (*bottom*); common violets (*facing page*)

favorite
flower
recipes

I remember the first time an artichoke was placed in front of me. I had never seen one, and a knife and fork looked woefully inadequate. "How do you eat it?" I asked my hostess. Over the years I have had a similar feeling when restaurants put flowers on my plate. Flower eating is not part of our culinary heritage, but in many other cultures, both ancient and modern, people grow up eating flowers without thinking it odd at all. The Japanese and Chinese put chrysanthemum blossoms in tea, Italians regularly use squash blossoms, and other Europeans have used roses and violets for centuries. In fact, much of the information in the Encyclopedia of Edible Flowers (page 29) was drawn from historical documents and ethnic cookbooks.

_____

Edible flowers (*top*) ready to garnish a buffet table full of salads include calendulas, chives, mustard flowers, and scented geraniums.

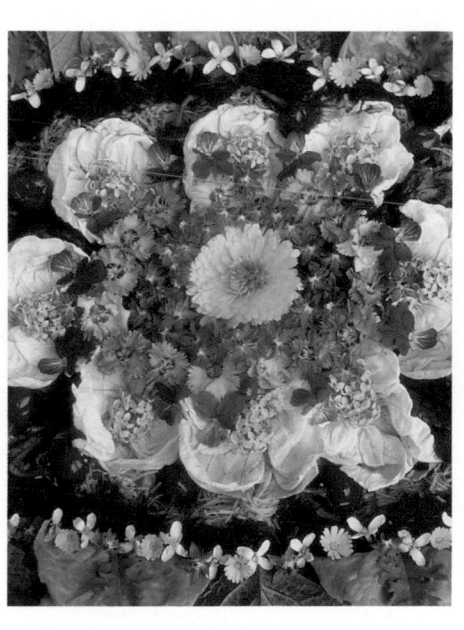

I gathered the following recipes partly from those sources, partly from some of this country's best cooking professionals, and partly from my own experience. Unfortunately, I couldn't begin to incorporate all the ways of preparing edible flowers, but you'll get a good foundation. You'll also discover that you can get very involved without using complicated cooking techniques and that the range of possibilities is

exhilarating. Even very simple uses of flowers can be quite spectacular—chopping up rose petals and incorporating them into sweet butter, for example, or decorating baked pears with white lilac florets. Consider making such dishes as baklava flavored with rose petal honey, herb pizza sprinkled with nasturtium and herb flowers, a wedding cake strewn with fresh violets or orange blossoms, or sorbet made with cottage pinks or apple blossoms.

Flowers in the kitchen are indisputably primarily decorative—their colors and shapes are truly spectacular additions. American cooks are beginning to think more and more about how food is presented and to subscribe to the belief that beautiful meals are more satisfying and life-enhancing than plain fare. Consider how much more festive and colorful are salads made with borage and nasturtium blossoms than those sporting the usual radish or red cabbage slices. Parsley has been done to death, so how about using mustard or scarlet runner bean blossoms instead? Or for an alternative to the usual frosting flowers on your next birthday cake, how about using violets or honeysuckle blossoms or large damask rose petals?

But eye appeal is not the only virtue of edible flowers. Many actually give us new flavors to cook with. Consider the rich aroma of roses, lavender, orange blossoms, or anise hyssop.

The "Encyclopedia of Edible Flowers" resolves the most important issue of which flowers are edible, but some fundamental questions remain: How are the flowers prepared for cooking? What parts are edible? Which flowers go with which dishes? First, taste some of the flowers to see if you like them. This step may seem obvious, but I've been served some pretty unpalatable flowers over the years—I'm sure the cooks hadn't tasted them beforehand. Pick the flowers in the cool of the clay, preferably in the morning. Put those with long stems in water; pick short-stemmed ones, such as borage and orange blossoms, no more than three or four hours ahead of time, put them between layers of damp paper towels or in a plastic bag, and refrigerate. Flowers, of course, are perishable and wilt in a warm place. And they'll bruise almost instantly if they're handled roughly.

Most cooks gently wash flowers before using them. Especially for candying, flowers must be thoroughly dry, so allow an hour or so for the flowers to dry. While washing your flowers, look for "critters," such as baby slugs, earwigs, and thrips, that might be hiding down in the petals. There are more places to hide in flowers than in vegetables, and many people get really upset when they see something crawl out of their salad.

With some flowers—such as roses, calendulas, tulips, chrysanthemums, and lavender—only the petals are edible. With others—Johnny-jump-ups, violets, and pea and runner bean blossoms—the whole flower can be eaten. Separate the petals just before you use them, as they wilt within minutes. Some flower petals, such as those of roses, dianthus, and marigolds, have a white part that can be quite bitter; remove it. Also remove the stamens, styles, and sepals of large flowers such as tulips, open lilies, and squash blossoms because they are usually too tough.

It is important for the flowers to fit the dish. While not an absolute rule, sweet flowers are best in or as garnishes to desserts and fruit dishes, and savory types are wonderful with soups, salads, and entrées. For example, use chive blossoms in sandwiches and on onion dishes, nasturtiums in salads, and mustard blossoms on ham-filled crepes. The sweet, floral taste of roses, violets, and apple blossoms goes well with cakes, puddings, and pies. Bee balm petals are rather floral and sweet but make a good garnish to a lemon-flavored fish sauce. Use discretion with garnishes; the flavor of the flower shouldn't overpower the dish. Lavender, for instance, is very strong, and a whole flower on a light cream soup would probably obliterate the taste of the soup. A few tiny lavender petals or mild calendula petals would be a subtle and elegant solution.

Use squash blossoms in crepes, light soups, and omelets. Steep lavender and apple blossoms as well as honeysuckle, anise hyssop, and violets in milk and then use the milk to make a custard for pies, puddings, ice cream, or for filling for cream puffs. Imagine floating-island pudding with a violet-flavored custard and meringues decorated with candied violets. Even more lusciously decadent is a Grand Marnier chocolate cake decorated with orange blossoms. Use flower butters on pasta, bread, tea sandwiches, and biscuits. Use candied flowers throughout the year on mousses, soufflés, chiffon and cream pies, chocolate truffles, petits fours, hors d'oeuvres, ice creams, iced teas, and all kinds of cakes.

Classic tea sandwiches (*left*) are filled with watercress and cream cheese. Blue violas and white watercress blossoms are tucked into the sandwiches and used to garnish the plate. Rose-scented geranium jelly can be used between layers of pound cake or piped into delicate rolled cookies to make little treats to serve at a shower or fancy party (*above*).

Flower Butters

Both savory and sweet butters can be made with flowers. Probably the most versatile savory butters are made from chive blossoms or nasturtium flowers. Serve these savory butters with a crisp French bread or melt them over vegetables, fish, or poultry. Or also add savory herbs, lemon juice, or other flavorings such as ground chipotle peppers or grated fresh ginger. Sweet flower butters can be made with roses, violets, lavender, and pineapple sage and are a treat on egg breads, sugar cookies, or as a mystery filling between layers of pound or sponge cake.

Nasturtium Butter

4 ounces unsalted butter (1 stick), room temperature

12 to 18 nasturtium flowers

2 to 4 fresh nasturtium leaves, or a few sprigs of fresh parsley

3 or 4 chive leaves (optional)

Chive Blossom Butter

4 ounces unsalted butter (1 stick), room temperature

10 to 12 large, barely open common chive flowers, florets (petal clusters) separated

2 small sprigs of fresh parsley, or 8 or 10 large chive leaves

Rose Butter

4 ounces unsalted butter (1 stick), room temperature

1 teaspoon superfine sugar, or finely granulated sugar (sometimes called bartenders' sugar)

¼ teaspoon almond extract

Generous handful of rose petals from the fragrant old-fashioned types, such as 'Belle of Portugal,' any of the rugosa roses and damasks, and the 'Eglantine' rose (enough to yield 2 tablespoons of chopped petals)

Making any flower butter involves the same process. First, remove the petals from the flowers and wash them well in cold water—check for critters. Gently pat them dry in a towel or dry them in a salad spinner. Using a very sharp knife, mince the flowers and any leaves. (Mincing is easier if you roll the blossoms into a small ball before cutting them.) Cut a stick of room-temperature butter into six or eight pieces and then mash them with a fork. When the butter is fairly soft, slowly incorporate any flavorings and the flowers and leaves. With a rubber spatula put the mixture into a small butter crock or decorative bowl. Refrigerate until serving time. Flower butters can be frozen in sealed containers for up to two months.

All three recipes make a little more than ½ cup.

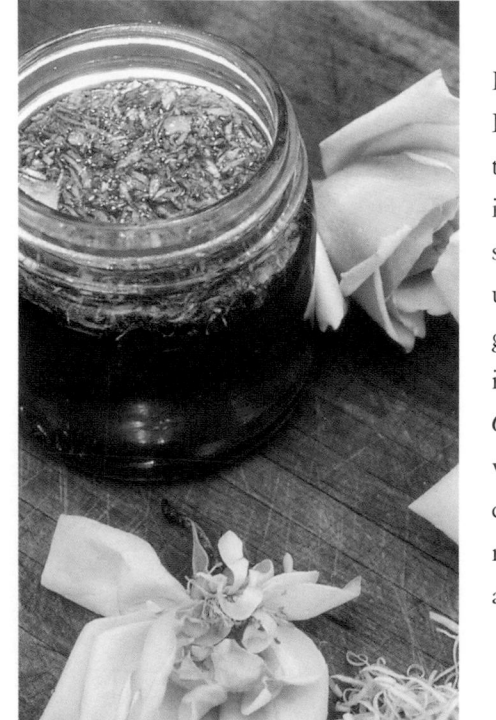

Sweet Things

Lavender Sugar

Making fragrant lavender sugar takes about a month. Use it to flavor cookies, lemonade, and hot or cold teas.

½ cup dried lavender leaves and
    flowers
2 cups superfine sugar, or fincly
    ground granulated sugar (some-
    times called bartenders' sugar)

In a jar with a tight lid, mix the dried lavender and the superfine sugar. Shake it up occasionally to equally distribute the sugar. After about three weeks to a month the oils of the lavender will have flavored the sugar sufficiently. Sift the mixture through a large strainer to remove the lavender. Store the sugar in its jar for up to a year.

Makes 2 cups.

Rose Petal Honey

Robin Sanders and Bruce Naftaly of Le Gourmand restaurant in Seattle use this honey to make baklava, transforming an already delicious dessert into something divine. They also suggest using this honey in other desserts, meat glazes, and tea. When using rose honey in your favorite baklava recipe (*Joy of Cooking* has one; eliminate the orange water, though), also sprinkle a few chopped honeyed rose petals on the nut mixture and use fresh or candied roses as garnish.

1 cup unsprayed rose petals,
    preferably the fragrant old-
    fashioned types, such as 'Belle
    of Portugal,' any of the rugosa
    roses, damasks, and the
    eglantine rose
1 cup honey

Rinse the rose petals briefly in cold water and dry them in a salad spinner. In a nonaluminum pan, slowly heat the honey until runny. With a wooden spoon stir in the rose petals, cover, and steep over extremely low heat for 45 minutes, stirring occasionally. Remove from heat and let cool for 15 minutes. Strain the honey through a fine sieve, and reserve petals for another use.

Makes about 1 cup.

Quick Rose-Scented Geranium Apple Jelly

This is one of Carole Saville's creations. Her favorite way to use the jelly is to make pound cake "sandwiches." If you want a more strongly flavored jelly, add another scented geranium leaf to the recipe.

¼ cup fresh rasp berries
3 large rose-scented geranium
    leaves
1 (10-ounce) jar apple jelly
Petals from 18 rose-scented
    geranium flowers

Place the raspberries in a strainer placed over a small bowl. With the back of a spoon mash the berries against the side of the strainer to extract the juice. Set the juice aside.

Wash and thoroughly dry the geranium leaves. Finely chop the leaves and tie them in a square of cheesecloth.

Pour the apple jelly into a saucepan and quickly bring it to a boil. Stir in the reserved raspberry juice, then add the bag of geranium leaves. Stir the mixture for 1 minute, then cover tightly, and remove from heat. Let the jelly cool for about 20 minutes. Uncover the pan and, with the back of a spoon, press the bag of geranium leaves against the side of the pan to extract all the juice. Discard the bag of geranium leaves. Stir in the geranium petals. Pour the still-warm jelly into a hot, sterilized jar. Put on the lid and allow the jelly to cool (it should take approximately an hour). Refrigerate and use within two weeks.

Makes 10 ounces.

Tip:

"I add an extract of roses to a standard angel food cake and cover with a pale pink icing. I then decorate the cake with fresh roses and violets and put rose geranium leaves around the base. I serve it with ice cream and a little bit of creme de cassis (a black-currant liqueur) so that everything is pale pink."

—Holly Shimizu, managing director of the Lewis Ginter Botanical Garden in Richmond, Virginia

Candied Flowers

Baby roses, Johnny-jump-ups, violets, violas, scented geraniums, orange blossoms, edible pea blossoms (not sweet peas, which are poisonous), and borage are all particularly well suited to candying.

Use candied flowers to decorate cakes, cookies, ice cream, and hors d'oeuvres. Wedding cakes are stunning covered with candied roses, and salmon canapés are dramatic decorated with candied pea blossoms. For an Art Deco presentation, cover a cake with marzipan icing, wrap it with blue French ribbon, and create a cluster of matte-finish blue-candied pansies.

In the cool of the morning on a dry day, select and cut flowers that are perfectly shaped and newly opened. Keep enough of their stems so you can put them in water and later hold them comfortably. Wash the flowers a few hours before working with them so they will be dry.

To candy flowers, you need a small paint brush, a bowl, cake rack, fork, finely ground granulated sugar (sometimes called bartenders' sugar or superfine sugar), and an egg white.

In a small bowl, beat an egg white only slightly. Holding a flower by its stem, gently paint the petals with a light coating of egg white, thoroughly covering the front and back because any part of the petal not covered will wither and discolor. Sprinkle the flowers with sugar, making sure to cover both sides of the petals thoroughly. An

To candy violets (*top*) or other edible flowers, first give them a light coating of egg white with a paint brush, being careful to completely cover the petals. With your fingers, lightly sprinkle extra-fine granulated sugar over the petals. Dry them on a rack in a very warm, dry place for a few days or in a dehydrator until firm. Once the flowers are dry (*bottom*), put them in a flat, dry container. Use the flowers to decorate cakes and cookies. Any alternative method is to use a paste mixture of confectioners' sugar and a little egg white. This mixture gives a matte finish to citrus blossoms and large flowers like dark-colored pansies. Paint this mixture on both sides of the petals.

When your flower is completely sugared, lay it on a cake rack and spread the petals in a natural position. After an hour or two move the flowers around so the petals won't stick to the rack. Put the flowers in a warm, dry place (I use my gas oven, with just the heat from its pilot light) or in a food dehydrator set on low. After a few days they should be fully dry; store them in a sealed tin. Some of the flowers will become deformed; discard them or break them up to use as a confetti. You can use your candied flowers immediately, but if you store them in a dry place, most varieties will keep for up to a year.

broken pieces of candied flowers can be used to sprinkle on confections as you would confetti, shown on the cake in the same photo, to the right. When you candy flowers, if you use confectioner's instead of granulated sugar you can achieve a mat finish on the flowers, giving them a delicate, old-fashioned look. The cake here (*far right*) has been garnished with yellow pansies that were treated in this manner.

Edible Flower Canapés

Edible flowers provide a striking palette with which to decorate food. With a small garden of edible flowers you can make your canapés look like edible art.

½ cup snipped fresh dill or chive leaves

1 pound natural cream cheese, softened

2 large loaves of dense sandwich or rustic-style unsliced bread, or 2 packages melba toast

A selection of edible flowers, 4 or 5 dozen: nasturtiums, borage, calendulas, pineapple sage, runner bean flowers, pansies, violas, violets, and mustard flowers

Herb leaves: sage, parsley, mint, dill, and basil

In a mixing bowl, add the chives and 3 tablespoons of water to the cream cheese and mix until smooth. If the mixture is too thick, add a little more water.

Trim the crusts off the bread and cut it into ⅓-inch-thick slices. Cut the slices into large squares or rectangles 2½ to 3½ inches wide. Spread the cream cheese mixture on the bread—approximately 1 tablespoon per square—and arrange the squares on cookie sheets. Cover them lightly with plastic wrap and refrigerate until ready to decorate.

Carefully wash the flowers and herbs and gently pat them dry on paper towels. Lay them out on damp paper towels and cover with plastic wrap. Refrigerate until ready to use, but not for more than a few hours.

Decorate each canapé square with an edible flower or two and an herb leaf or two. Re-cover the canapés lightly with plastic wrap and refrigerate until serving time. The canapés may be done a few hours in advance, but do not prepare them any earlier, or the garnishes will wilt.

Put a paper doily on a decorative tray, place decorated squares on the tray, and serve.

Appetizers for 6 to 8 people.

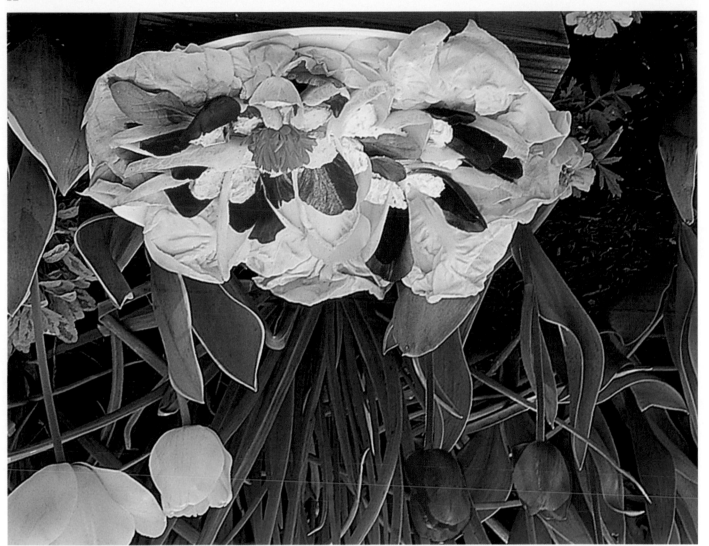

Tulip and Endive Appetizer

If you can spare a few tulips in full bloom for an appetizer plate, you will set the party atwitter.

Inside leaves from 2 medium heads of Bibb lettuce

4 or 5 large tulip flowers of different colors

2 or 3 Belgian endives

For the filling:

4 ounces chèvre cheese

2 to 3 tablespoons heavy cream

Flavorings: minced pimiento strips; finely chopped nasturtium or violet petals; or minced fresh herbs such as fennel, tarragon, chives, and sorrel

Arrange a bed of Bibb lettuce leaves on a large serving platter.

Remove the petals from the tulips and gently wash them. Place them on paper towels to dry. Cut the root end off the endives and separate the leaves. Cover and refrigerate the lettuce, tulip petals, and endives if you're not serving them right away.

To make the filling: In a small bowl, use a fork to break up the chèvre, working in a few tablespoons of cream. Use enough cream to make the chèvre workable. With a fork incorporate the flavorings to taste.

To assemble the appetizers: Lay out about 18 endive leaves. Top them with 1 or 2 tulip petals. At the base of each petal place ⅓ teaspoon or so of the chèvre mixture. Arrange the appetizers on the bed of Bibb lettuce and serve.

Makes 18 to 24.

Citrus Dip for Begonia Blossoms

The slightly crisp texture and sweet citrus flavor of begonias can be a spectacular ice-breaking appetizer. The blossoms come in many splashy colors, and a platterful makes a lovely centerpiece for a buffet table.

1 tablespoon honey
1 tablespoon frozen orange juice concentrate
1 teaspoon orange zest
½ teaspoon lemon zest
½ cup nonfat yogurt
4 large organically grown tuberous begonia flowers

In a small bowl, combine the honey, orange juice concentrate, and orange and lemon zests. Add the yogurt and mix well. Pour the yogurt mixture into a small decorative bowl, cover it with plastic wrap, and refrigerate until ready to serve.

Just before serving, gently wash the begonia blossoms and remove each of the petals at its base. Place the bowl of flavored yogurt on a large platter and arrange the petals in a decorative pattern around the bowl. Serve the appetizer within the hour to prevent the petals from wilting.

Serves 4 to 6.

Pineapple Sage Salsa

Cathy Barash, executive garden editor of Meredith Books, created this recipe while visiting when my pineapple sage was in bloom. This salsa is a delicious accompaniment to fish, such as grilled swordfish or tuna, or serve it on a bed of baby greens as an appetizer.

1 pineapple, peeled, cored, and cut into small bite-size chunks
1 sweet yellow bell pepper, finely diced (about 1 cup)
½ cup Vidalia or Walla Walla onion, finely chopped
2 tablespoons Rose's sweetened lime juice
½ teaspoon ground dried ancho or other mild chile pepper
½ cup pineapple sage flowers, measured, then coarsely chopped

In a glass or stainless-steel (nonreactive) bowl, toss together all the ingredients. Cover and refrigerate for at least 6 hours to allow the flavors to meld.

Makes about 2 cups.

Ricotta-Stuffed Zucchini Flowers

This recipe was created by Vicki Sebastiani, famous for her garden, her cooking, and her family winery, Viansa Winery and Italian Marketplace in Sonoma, California. The proportions vary according to the number and sizes of the flowers. A word of caution: sometimes bees get trapped in the squash flowers.

1 pound ricotta cheese

1 onion, minced

½ cup toasted almonds, or pine nuts, finely chopped

½ cup grated Asiago (or Parmesan) cheese

½ teaspoon freshly ground black pepper

1 teaspoon seasoned salt

2 tablespoons minced fresh basil

2 tablespoons minced fresh Italian parsley

1 teaspoon melted butter

Approximately 20 to 30 medium zucchini (or any other squash) flowers, freshly picked

Garnish: nasturtium flowers

Rinse the flowers. Mix together all the ingredients except the butter and flowers. With the filling at room temperature, use a pastry tube to carefully stuff the flowers; do not overfill them.

Drizzle the melted butter over the flowers and microwave them on medium power for 3 minutes, or bake at 350°F in a regular oven for 15 minutes. Be careful not to overcook the flowers or allow the filling to ooze out.

Arrange the stuffed flowers on a serving platter. Garnish with nasturtiums stuffed with leftover filling.

Serves 10 as an appetizer.

Sage Tempura

Ron Ottobre developed this flashy and incredibly tasty appetizer while he was executive chef at Mudd's Restaurant in San Ramon, California.

⅔ cups cornmeal

2 cups unbleached flour

4 tablespoons cornstarch

2 tablespoons baking powder

2 tablespoons sugar

2 teaspoons salt

½ cup whole milk

2 eggs, beaten

2 tablespoons peanut oil

Oil for frying

16 (4-inch) lengths of sage in bloom (flowers and leaves)

In a large bowl, sift together the cornmeal, flour, cornstarch, baking powder, sugar, and salt. In a separate bowl, whisk together 1 cup of water, the milk, eggs, and peanut oil. Gradually whisk together the two mixtures. In a heavy frying pan, heat about 1 inch oil until a dollop of batter dropped in sizzles and bubbles. Dip the sage into the batter and drop into the oil (depending on the size of the frying pan, you can usually cook about 6 at a time without cooling down the oil too much). When they're lightly browned on one side, turn the sage over, and cook the other side. Remove to paper towels or brown paper to drain. Serve immediately with your favorite dipping sauce, or reheat in the oven the next day.

Serves 4.

Flower Confetti Salad

Chartreuse butter lettuces and the warm colors of flower petals can dress up an everyday salad or start off a festive meal. A salad can be especially dramatic when prepared at the table. Pick flowers as close to serving time as possible. Put the stems in a glass of water and refrigerate.

For the salad:

1 large, or 2 small, heads of Bibb lettuce

1 large handful of mixed baby greens

6 to 8 edible flowers such as nasturtiums, calendulas, violas, pansies, rose petals, or chrysanthemums

For the dressing:

2 tablespoons rice-wine or champagne vinegar

Salt and freshly ground black pepper

1 teaspoon frozen white grape juice or apple juice concentrate

3 or 4 tablespoons extra-virgin olive oil

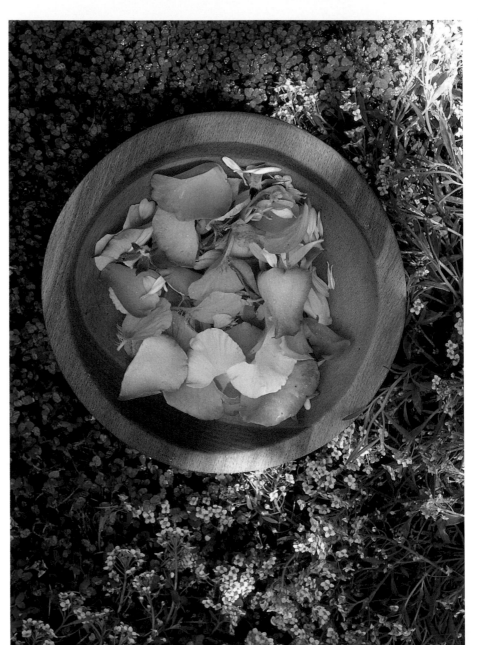

To make the salad: Wash the lettuce and baby greens and dry them in a salad spinner or gently pat them dry with paper towels. In a large salad bowl, break the lettuce leaves into bite-size pieces and add baby greens. If not serving immediately, cover the bowl lightly with plastic wrap and refrigerate.

To make the dressing: In a small bowl, combine the vinegar, salt, pepper, and juice concentrate. Whisk in the oil until blended.

Wash the flowers gently, lightly pat them dry with paper towels, and gently pull off the petals. In a small bowl, stir the petals to mix the colors and make a confetti. You should have about ⅓ cup of loosely packed petals. Stir the dressing, pour 3 or 4 tablespoons over the lettuce and greens, and toss. Add more dressing if needed, but be careful not to overwhelm the salad. Divide the salad equally among four salad plates. Scatter a small handful of flower-petal confetti over each individual salad and serve.

Serves 4.

Wild Violet Salad

Violets are tasty and very nutritious and grow so easily they can become a pest. But what a pest. My violets give me greens and flowers from February to May. Look your garden over and see what other unusual greens can be harvested: pea shoots from edible peas, miner's lettuce, chickweed, or tiny young dandelion leaves.

Caution: Make sure you can positively identify your greens and that none have been sprayed with toxic chemicals.

For the salad:

1 large handful of baby mesclun greens
1 handful of young violet leaves
1 small head of romaine or butter lettuce
6 or 8 pea tendrils (tender shoots at the ends of the vines)
8 to 10 violet flowers

For the dressing:

1½ to 2 tablespoons balsamic or red wine vinegar
1 teaspoon honey
Salt and freshly ground black pepper
2 tablespoons extra-virgin olive oil
1 tablespoon hazelnut or almond oil

Wash the mesclun greens, violet leaves, lettuces, and pea tendrils well in a large amount of water in the sink or in the bowl of a salad spinner. Vigorously

slosh the greens up and down. Repeat the process two or three times until the water is completely clear. Spin the greens in the salad spinner or pat them dry with paper towels. Break the lettuce leaves and pea tendrils into bite-size pieces. Put the mesclun, lettuce, violet leaves, and pea tendrils in a salad bowl, cover, and refrigerate until serving time. Gently wash the flowers. Refrigerate in a glass of water until just before serving.

To make the dressing: In a small container, combine the vinegar, honey, salt, and pepper and with a fork or wire whisk blend in the oils. Drizzle the dressing over the greens and toss. Remove the stems from the flowers, add the flowers to the salad, and serve.

Serves 4.

Baby Shower Petal Salad

This salad can be expanded to feed a large crowd. Plan on one large handful of salad greens per person and approximately ½ cup of dressing for six people. This is a great vehicle for showing off your garden, so include unusual greens like orach, ornamental cabbages, and violet leaves, as well as herbs like chervil and borage. Choose edible flowers in the pink, blue, and white range for a garnish.

For the salad:
6 handfuls of mixed salad greens
1 handful of baby leaves of fancy
    greens: orach, violets, ornamenttal
cabbage, mizuna, tatsoi,
    amaranth, and mâche
6 to 8 large colorful ornamental
    cabbage leaves

For the dressing:
2 to 3 tablespoons champagne
    vinegar or white-wine vinegar
Salt and freshly ground black pepper
1 small garlic clove, finely minced
    (optional)
4 or 5 tablespoons extra-virgin
    olive oil
1 tablespoon finely chopped fresh
    mint or basil
Garnish: baby rose petals; strawberry
    blossoms; borage; violas;
    pansies; violets; dianthus;
    apple, pear, and plum blossoms;
    and chives

Wash the greens well, dry them in a salad spinner, and arrange them in a large bowl. Place the large leaves of ornamental cabbage around the outside of the bowl.

In a small bowl, combine the vinegar, salt, pepper, and garlic if desired. Whisk in the oil. Add the herbs and stir.

Just before serving, sprinkle the dressing over the greens. Arrange the flowers over the salad and serve immediately.

Serves 6.

Mardi Gras Salad with Pecans

For an exciting winter dish, try a salad celebrating Mardi Gras. In New Orleans the colors of Mardi Gras are gold, green, and blue. Since salad greens and cool-season edible flowers are at their best in mild climates during this February festival, a salad made with fresh greens at their peak and edible flowers in colors to match the theme is a real show-off dish and adds style to the celebration.

For the dressing:

3 tablespoons balsamic vinegar
Salt and freshly ground black pepper
5 tablespoons extra-virgin olive oil
1 to 2 tablespoons minced fresh lemon thyme or spearmint
1 small garlic clove, pressed

For the salad:

1 head butter lettuce
½ head of romaine
1 handful of fresh baby spinach leaves, or mature spinach
½ cup whole pecans broken into bite-size pieces
12 to 20 gold nasturtiums and calendulas, and blue and gold pansies and violas

To make the dressing: In a small bowl combine the vinegar, salt, and pepper, blend in the oil, and add the thyme and garlic.

To make the salad: Wash the greens and break them into bite-size pieces. Place the greens and pecans in a large salad bowl.

Gently wash the flowers. Remove the petals and put them in a small bowl.

To serve, whisk the vinaigrette well, pour it over the greens, and toss gently. Adjust seasonings if necessary after the dressing is tossed with the greens. Just before serving, sprinkle flower petals over the salad.

Serves 4 to 6.

Poor Man's Pilaf

The perfume of the spices and the beauty of the flower petals makes this a special dish. To obtain the most color from the petals, mince the petals well before adding them to the rice. Serve with a salad for a light supper or as an interesting side dish.

About 15 cardamom pods
⅛ teaspoon cumin seeds
⅛ teaspoon coriander seeds
2 tablespoons vegetable oil
1 large onion, finely chopped
1½ cups basmati rice
1-inch-diameter sheaf of spaghetti, broken into 3-inch pieces
3½ cups homemade or low-sodium chicken stock or vegetable stock
1 cup cubed carrots
¾ cup plus 2 tablespoons calendula petals, divided
½ teaspoon ground red pepper
1 cup fresh or frozen petit pois
½ cup sliced almonds
2 tablespoons safflower petals

Remove the outer shell of the cardamom pods and take out the seeds. (You need ⅛ teaspoon.) In a dry sauté pan, toast the cardamom, cumin, and coriander seeds over low heat until they start to perfume the air. Remove them from the pan and grind them with a mortar and pestle or in a spice grinder. (I use a coffee grinder that I keep just for spices.) Set the spice mixture aside.

In a large sauté pan with a lid, heat the oil, and over medium-low heat sauté the onion until translucent, about 7 minutes. Add the rice and spaghetti and sauté over low heat until they start to brown. Add the chicken stock and the carrots to the pan carefully, as the oil may splatter. Chop ¾ cup of the ca-

lendula petals and add them to the rice mixture. Add the spice mixture and the pepper to the rice and stir. Cover and simmer on low heat for about 20 to 25 minutes, until the rice is tender and the liquid has been absorbed. Add the peas and cook until done, 1 or 2 more minutes. Take the pan off the heat, stir in the almonds, and transfer to a serving bowl. Sprinkle on the safflower petals and the remaining 2 tablespoons calendula petals and serve.

Serves 4 to 6.

Stir-Fried Beef with Anise Hyssop

This simple and delicious dish from Renee Shepherd, of Renee's Garden, uses anise hyssop to add a subtle flavor that enhances all the other ingredients. Serve over fluffy white rice.

½ cup chopped anise hyssop flowers
    and leaves
⅓ cup soy sauce
1 tablespoon brown sugar
2 tablespoons sherry
1 pound flank steak, cut across the
    grain into strips 3 inches long
    and ¼ inch wide
2 tablespoons vegetable oil
3 tablespoons chopped scallions
¼ cup chicken broth
2 teaspoons cornstarch dissolved in
    2 teaspoons water

In a bowl, combine the anise hyssop flowers and leaves, soy sauce, brown sugar, and sherry. Pour the mixture over the steak strips and marinate for several hours.

Remove the meat from the marinade, reserving the remaining sauce. In a wok or large skillet, heat the oil and stir-fry the meat quickly over medium-high heat until brown, about 5 minutes. Add the scallions, the chicken broth, and the marinade and heat through. Stir in the cornstarch mixture until the sauce thickens. Garnish with flowers if desired.

Serves 4 to 6.

Grilled Swordfish with Rosemary

This recipe from Carole Saville blends the richness of swordfish with the assertiveness of rosemary. It works equally well if you broil the swordfish.

- ¼ cup fresh rosemary leaves and soft stems, plus 4 teaspoons, divided
- 1 cup extra-virgin olive oil
- 2 tablespoons fresh lemon juice
- ¼ teaspoon salt
- Ground red pepper
- 4 swordfish steaks, 1 inch thick (about 5 ounces each)
- Garnish: 4 teaspoons finely chopped rosemary, rosemary flowers if in bloom, and lemon wedges

Finely chop the rosemary. In a small bowl, rub the rosemary with the bottom of a glass to bruise it. In a large, deep plate, mix the olive oil, lemon juice, salt, ground red pepper, and rosemary and stir to combine.

Rinse the swordfish and pat it dry. Turn each steak over in the marinade to coat well. Cover the plate and refrigerate for 1 hour, turning the swordfish once.

Grill the fish over medium flame, turning after 5 minutes. Grill until the flesh is opaque when cut in the thickest part, about 5 more minutes. Remove to four warmed plates. Sprinkle 1 teaspoon of chopped rosemary over each serving. Garnish with lemon wedges. Serve immediately.

Serves 4.

Rose Petal Syrup

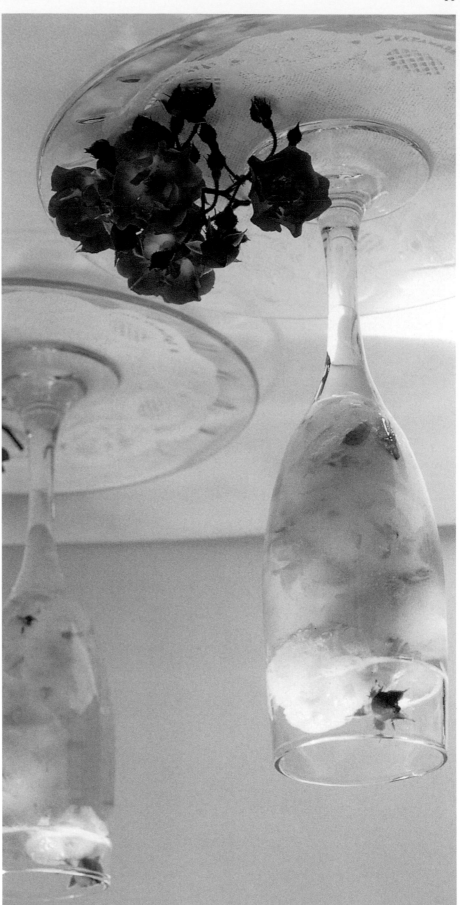

This versatile syrup can be used on crepes or pancakes, drizzled over sponge cake, or used in sorbets. My favorite roses to use are 'Belle of Portugal,' 'Abraham Darby,' and the spicy *Rosa rugosa alba*. Try your own varieties for flavor. Some are sensational, others metallic or bitter tasting. If the white bases of the petals are bitter, remove them.

Caution: Use only roses that have not been sprayed with commercial chemicals. Diners allergic to sulfur should be particularly careful, as organic gardeners often use sulfur to control rose diseases.

2 cups rose petals
⅔ cup sugar

Wash the petals and dry them in a salad spinner. Check for insects. Chop the petals very fine. In a medium saucepan, bring 1 cup of water to a boil and stir in the sugar. When the sugar is melted, add the petals. Remove the syrup from the heat and cover it tightly. Let it steep overnight. Taste the syrup the next day, and if the flavor is not strong enough, reheat the syrup, add more petals, and let it steep overnight again. You can store the syrup in the refrigerator for up to two weeks—freeze it for longer storage. Makes 1 cup.

Rose Petal Sorbet

1 cup rose syrup (see page 86 for recipe)
1 bottle of late harvest Gewürztraminer grape juice
4 perfect large rose blossoms
1 egg white

Micheal Isles, chef/instructor in Chico, California, created this fabulous treat. Make the syrup at least two days before making the sorbet.

A day before serving, combine the syrup and grape juice in an ice cream maker. Follow the manufacturer's directions for making sorbet. Once the sorbet is done, freeze it in an airtight container for 24 hours. You can get away with only 3 hours as an absolute minimum.

To serve, choose four perfect large roses, remove the centers, spread them open, and secure them to the middle of the plates or dishes with a little egg white. Just before serving, place a scoop of sorbet in each rose. The sorbet may also be served in sherbet glasses or floating in champagne in fancy long-stemmed goblets.

Serves 4 to 6.

Lavender Ice Cream

14 ounces whole milk
1½ ounces fresh lavender flowers and leaves
2 ounces crystallized ginger, minced
1 cup granulated sugar

This recipe was inspired by Chef David Schy when he was chef at the El Encanto Hotel in Santa Barbara. He served this ice cream at a seminar, and participants were reduced to bickering like children over who had the most.

3 egg yolks

2 cups cold heavy whipping cream

In a saucepan, slowly heat the milk to approximately 200°F. Remove from heat, add the lavender flowers, and steep for 15 minutes. While it's still warm, strain the milk through a cheesecloth. Add the ginger and sugar to the milk. Place the egg yolks in a small bowl and pour in half of the milk mixture. Stir the mixture with a spoon, then pour it back into the saucepan. Place the pan over low heat and cook until the mixture is approximately 200°F. Remove the saucepan from the heat and stir in the whipping cream. Refrigerate the mixture until it is well chilled, then process in any ice cream machine.

Makes 1 quart.

Tangelo and Kiwi Salad with Orange Blossoms

This citrus salad is lovely to look at, and the flavors are both familiar yet slightly different. Taste your citrus petals before adding them to the dressing. Expect some bitterness; but if they are very harsh, try blossoms from another tree. The point of adding a few citrus blossoms to the dressing is to infuse the tangelo juice with a lovely aroma and to deepen the citrus flavor.

6 medium tangelos, divided, or 3 tangelos and 1 cup of bottled fresh tangerine juice

1 tablespoon fresh lemon juice

5 lemon, tangerine, or orange blossoms, divided

1 tablespoon honey (optional)

2 kiwifruit

Squeeze 3 of the tangelos and put the juice (or the bottled tangerine juice) in a medium bowl. Add the lemon juice and the petals of 3 of the orange blossoms. If the tangelos are not very sweet, add a tablespoon of honey. Peel and section the remaining 3 tangelos, peel and slice the kiwifruit, add them to the juice mixture, and stir to cover the fruit. Refrigerate for a few hours.

To serve, divide the fruit among four serving dishes. Pour the tangelo juice over the fruit and garnish with the remaining citrus blossom petals.

Serves 4.

68

Scented Geranium, Crème Fraîche, and Strawberries

Carole Saville, author of *Exotic Herbs*, has perfected cooking with scented geraniums—this is one of her recipes.

1 tablespoon finely minced rose-scented geranium leaves

3 tablespoons granulated sugar, divided

1 cup crème fraîche (see Note)

2 pints strawberries

Garnish: scented geranium flowers

In a small bowl, combine the scented geranium leaves, 2 tablespoons of sugar, and crème fraîche. Cover the bowl with plastic wrap and refrigerate for 48 hours. Scrape the crème fraîche into a large, fine-mesh sieve, and with the back of a spoon push it through and into another bowl. Discard the geranium leaves. Cover the crème fraîche with plastic wrap and return it to the refrigerator until ready to serve. Wash and hull the strawberries. Cut large ones into slices. Sprinkle with remaining 1 tablespoon sugar. Divide the strawberries among four small glass cups or bowls. Spoon the scented crème fraîche over each serving. Garnish with scented geranium flowers.

Serves 4.

Note: Crème fraîche is readily available in France, but is still a bit expensive and hard to find here. A good approximation can easily be made at home.

Place 1 cup heavy cream and 1 tablespoon buttermilk in a small bowl. Stir well, cover the bowl with plastic wrap, and leave the mixture at room temperature until it thickens slightly, about 12 to 24 hours depending on the temperature. Once it is thickened, refrigerate the crème fraîche until you are ready to use it. It will keep in the refrigerator for about a week.

desserts

Tea Cake with Anise Hyssop and Lemon

Another recipe from Renee Shepherd. The combination of anise and lemon will especially please those who do not like things too sweet. This bread keeps well and actually tastes best after being wrapped in foil overnight.

2 cups all-purpose flour
1 tablespoon baking powder
½ teaspoon salt
½ cup butter, room temperature
½ cup granulated sugar
Grated zest of 1 lemon
⅓ to ½ cup anise hyssop flowers, finely chopped
2 eggs, beaten
½ cup fresh lemon juice
½ cup chopped walnuts

Grease and flour a bread or loaf pan. Heat the oven to 350°F.

Sift together the flour, baking powder, and salt. In another bowl, with a hand mixer cream the butter with the sugar until fluffy. Then add the lemon zest, flowers, and eggs and beat the mixture just until thoroughly combined. Stir in the lemon juice. Gradually mix in the flour mixture and walnuts, until blended. Spoon the mixture into the pan and bake for 50 to 55 minutes. Let the cake cool on a rack.

Makes 1 loaf.

Lavender Shortbreads

Shortbread cookies lend themselves to all sorts of special flavor variations. Here I use lavender, but rose geraniums would be tasty too. Shortbread cookie stamps are available from some specialty baking-supply houses.

2 cups unsalted butter, room temperature
1 cup "Lavender Sugar" (see recipe, page 71)
½ teaspoon salt
4 cups all-purpose flour
2 teaspoons dried lavender blossoms

To make the shortbread: Using the paddle attachment on a stand mixer, blend the butter, lavender sugar, and salt on a low to medium speed until light and fluffy, about 10 minutes. Work in the flour gradually, scraping the bowl occasionally to blend all the ingredients well. Mix in the lavender blossoms. Shape the dough into a ball, wrap it in plastic wrap, and refrigerate it for at least 2 hours.

To shape the shortbread: If you're using a cookie stamp, cut the dough into golf-ball-size pieces. Roll each piece into a ball with your floured hands, then press it with the lightly floured stamp. Gently remove the stamp and place the formed dough on a cookie sheet lined with parchment paper.

If you don't have a stamp, roll out the dough on a floured board to about ½ inch thick. Using a cookie cutter or a 3-inch-diameter water glass, cut out circles and place them on a parchment-lined cookie sheet. Score each cookie with the tines of a fork a few times, making a pleasing pattern. You can also cut the dough into equal rectangles instead of circles.

Refrigerate the formed cookies for 30 minutes before baking them.

Preheat the oven to 300°F. Bake the shortbread for 25 to 30 minutes, or until it is pale golden but not brown.

Makes about 2 dozen cookies.

appendix A
planting and
maintenance

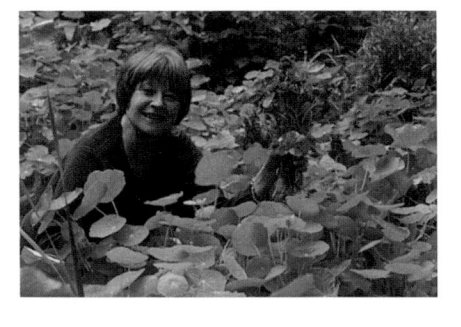

Covered in this section are the basics of soil preparation, starting seeds, transplanting, fertilizing, composting, mulching, watering and irrigation, and maintaining most annual, perennial, and woody, edible flowering plants.

Edible flowers are produced by many types of plants. Some, like nasturtiums and calendulas, are annuals. Others, like daylilies, chrysanthemums, dianthus, and many of the flowering herbs, are perennials and hence stay in the garden for a number of years. There are also the "woody" plants, such as apple trees, redbuds, and citrus trees, which might live as long as 100 years. And then there are the roses, which while usually classified as a woody shrub, I put in a category by themselves, as they are such a quirky lot. Each type of plant needs its own planning and planting treatment, and maintenance techniques differ too. A number of these plants, like the citrus and pineapple guava, are quite tender; although they can be grown in a greenhouse, only planting them in the ground in a suitable climate is addressed here, since indoor growing is a science of its own and beyond the scope of this book. The seeds for some annual and perennial edible flowers may need to be started indoors weeks before setting them out in the garden. Refer to "Starting Seeds" for guidelines on starting your seeds early.

Trees and Shrubs—
The Woody Plants
Planting

This section covers pineapple guava, elderberry, redbud, lilac, lemon, orange, and apple trees. Since these plantings are permanent, you need to give a lot of thought to where you plant them. Will they get too large for the location? Is the soil in the area well drained? Is there enough sunlight in the chosen spot? Most woody plants need fast-draining soil and at least six hours of midday sun. Even though homeowners want to plant them in a lawn, they never grow very well surrounded by grass: they must compete for nutrients and water, are damaged by mowers and trimmers, and, if the lawn needs constant irrigation, they eventually develop a number of diseases.

Once you've decided on where to put your tree or shrub, it's time to plant. Woody plants are best planted in the spring when they are most available in nurseries and when they will have a long season to get established before winter cold sets in. Apple trees are available bare root, that is, when they are dormant and the roots are wrapped for protection, but without soil, or in containers. Other trees and shrubs are usually sold only in five-gallon containers.

To prepare the soil for your tree or shrub, dig a hole that is double the width of the root ball and six inches deeper. Mix in a cup or so of bonemeal around the bottom and rough up the sides of the hole with a spade or digging fork. Mix in half a wheelbarrowful of organic matter, but only if the soil is light and sandy. (Contrary to past recommendations to amend the planting hole in heavy soils with copious amounts of organic matter, we now know that the roots of woody plants seldom leave amended fluffy soil to venture out into dense native soils. Instead, they remain confined to the planting hole. When the soil is not amended, the roots extend far into the parent soil.) Examine the root ball. Use a knife or sharp spade to cut through any thick mat of roots on the sides and bottom. Shovel some of the soil back in the hole and place the tree or shrub in the hole an inch or so higher than it was in the container. Straighten the roots out onto the backfill in the hole. Shovel the soil back in the hole and gently tamp the soil in place with your foot. Build up a small watering basin and water the plant in well by filling the basin full of water three or four times. Apply a mulch of organic matter at least three inches deep and at least six inches away from the trunk, to prevent the crown of the tree (where the bark meets the roots) from staying moist and possibly rotting. Keep the newly planted tree fairly moist for the first month and then start to taper off with the watering. In rainy climates water the tree if it rains less than once a week. In arid climates water deeply with at least one inch of water a week in hot weather. Drip irrigation is ideal for this purpose.

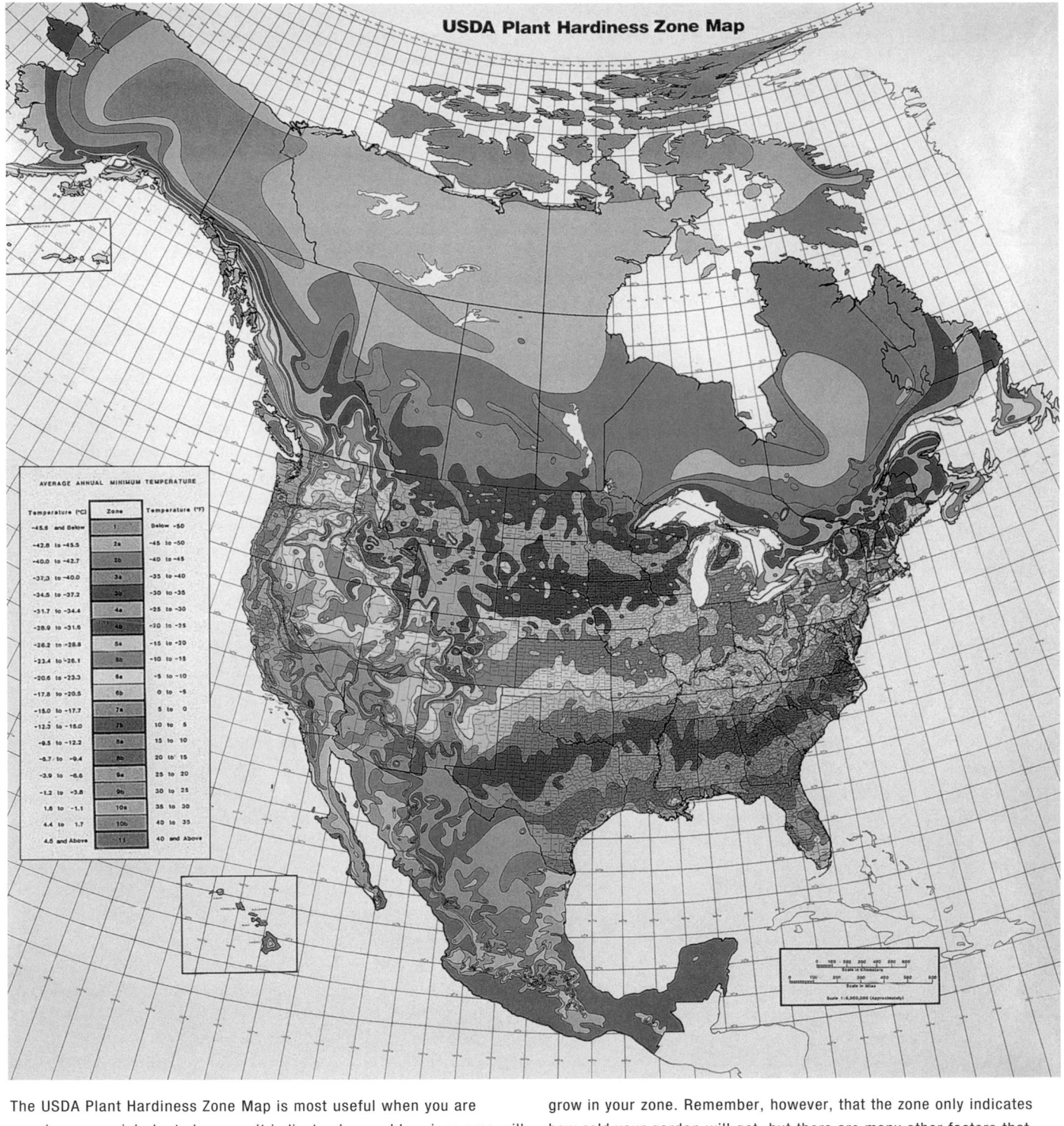

The USDA Plant Hardiness Zone Map is most useful when you are growing perennial plants because it indicates how cold a given area will be during an average winter. In order to use the map, locate your geographical area and consult the color code that indicates which zone you are in. When you select plants for your garden, choose ones that grow in your zone. Remember, however, that the zone only indicates how cold your garden will get, but there are many other factors that affect the health of your plants, namely summer highs and your area's soil type.

93

Maintaining Woody Plants

The maintenance of trees and shrubs differs for each species. See the information in the Encyclopedia of Edible Flowers for specific information; only the generalities are covered here. Woody plants need the most care in the first five years, when they are getting established. Young trees will need pruning to give them a well-formed shape; depending on the species, they may need pruning for optimum fruit production. They also need protection from cold in winter if they are tender, weeds removed from under the canopy of the tree, and an annual application of a well-balanced fertilizer such as fish meal or chicken manure in the spring. Throughout their lifetime they will grow best with a spring mulch, weed removal, and supplemental water during periods of drought.

Annuals, Perennials, Roses, and Vegetables

Installing a New Garden Bed

If you are planning a new garden area in which to plant annual and perennial flowers, plus a few vegetables, or you are installing a rose garden, the soil must be prepared more thoroughly. These plants need rich soil filled with organic matter and great drainage. To prepare the soil for a new garden, first remove large rocks and weeds. Dig out any perennial weeds and grasses, making sure to get out all the roots (including all those little pieces). It's tedious but will save you lots of work in the long run, as they usually come back—unfortunately up through your new plants. If you are taking up part of a lawn, the sod needs to be removed. If it is a small area, this can be done with a flat spade. Removing large sections, though, warrants renting a sod cutter. Next, when the soil is not too wet, spade over the area. Then cover it with three or four inches of compost (or other organic matter such as leaf mold or well-aged manure). Add even more compost if you live in a hot, humid climate where heat burns the compost at an accelerated rate, or if you have very alkaline, very sandy, or very heavy clay soil. Most plants grow best in a soil pH between 6 and 7, so add lime at

this time if your soil is acidic, following the directions on the package. Incorporate the ingredients thoroughly by turning over the soil with a spade. Add some bonemeal and work it into the top eight inches of soil, at the rate of 4 cups per 100 square feet. If your garden is large or the soil is very hard to work, you might use a rototiller to turn the soil. (When you put in a garden for the first time, a rototiller can be very helpful. However, research has shown that continued use of tillers is hard on soil structure and quickly burns up valuable organic matter if used regularly.) If you can do this soil preparation a few weeks before you plant, so much the better.

Finally, grade and rake the area. Make paths at least 3 feet wide through your garden so you can care for and harvest the flowers. Because of all the added materials, the beds will now be elevated above the paths—which further helps drainage. Slope the sides of the beds so that loose soil will not be washed or knocked onto the paths. Some gardeners add a brick or stone edging to outline the beds. Some sort of gravel, brick, stone, or mulch is needed on the paths to forestall weed growth, to give a strong design to your garden, and most important, to prevent your feet from getting wet and muddy.

Once the beds are prepared, it is planting time. I obtain my edible flower plants in different ways. Many of the annual flowers and vegetables I start from seeds. Plants like nasturtiums, calendulas, arugula, and marigolds are easily started from seeds, and radishes can be obtained no other way. Sometimes I buy my plants from nurseries if they have the varieties I want or if I'm late getting seeds started. Most perennials I purchase from local or mail-order nurseries, and plants that divide easily like chives and daylilies I usually get as divisions from a neighbor's plant. I find starting from seeds gives me lots of options with many fun varieties. Whereas the local nursery might carry one or two varieties of nasturtiums or calendulas, I might find a dozen varieties in a mail-order catalog.

Starting from Seeds

You can grow most annual and many perennial edible flowers from seeds. They

can be started indoors in flats or other well-drained containers or outdoors in a cold frame, or with some easily started annuals like nasturtiums and calendulas, directly in the garden. Starting seeds inside is usually preferable, as it gives your seedlings a warm and safe start.

The cultural needs of seeds vary widely among species. Still, some basic rules apply to most seeding procedures. First, whether you are starting seeds in the ground or in a container, make sure you have a loose, water-retentive soil that drains well. Good drainage is important because seeds can get waterlogged, and too much water can lead to "damping off," a fungal disease that kills seedlings at the soil line. Commercial starting mixes are usually best since they have been sterilized to remove weed seeds; however, the quality varies greatly from brand to brand, and I find most lack enough nitrogen, so I water with a weak solution of fish emulsion when I plant the seeds, and again every few weeks.

Smooth the soil surface and plant the seeds at the recommended depth. Pat down the seeds, and water carefully to make the seed bed moist but not soggy. When starting seeds outside, protect the seedbed with bird netting to keep out critters. If slugs and snails are a problem, circle the area with diatomaceous earth to keep them away, and go out at night with a flashlight to catch any that cross the barrier. If you are starting edible flowers in containers, put the seedling tray in a warm place to help seeds germinate more quickly.

When starting seeds inside, once they have germinated it's imperative that they immediately be given a quality source of light. A greenhouse, sunporch, greenhouse window, or south-facing window with no overhang will suffice, provided that it is warm. If one is not available, use fluorescent lights, which are available from home-supply stores or from specialty mail-order houses.

Keep the soil moist and, if you have seeded thickly and have crowded plants, thin the seedlings. It's less damaging to do so with small scissors. Cut the little plants out, leaving the remaining seedlings an inch or so apart. Do not transplant your seedlings until they have their second set of true leaves (the first leaves that sprout from a seed are called seed leaves and usually look different from the later true leaves). If the seedlings are tender, wait until all danger of frost is past before you set them out. Young plants started indoors or in a greenhouse should be "hardened off" before they are planted in the garden—that is, they should be put outside in a sheltered place for a few days in their containers to let them get used to the differences in temperature, humidity, and air movement.

Transplanting

Place the plants in their containers where they are to be planted. When planting a garden of annual flowers, vegetables, or perennials, choose short species and varieties for the front of the beds and tall ones for the back. Step back and see how you like the layout, and then fine-tune the arrangement. (The single biggest mistake we all make is not to allow enough room for the plant to spread to its maximum size.)

Now begin to plant. Before setting out transplants in the garden, check to see if a mat of roots has formed at the bottom of the root ball. I open it up so the roots won't continue to grow in a tangled mass. Even though the garden bed has been well prepared and by this time lots of organic matter and bonemeal have been added, for the heavy-feeding broccoli, mustard, and squash, I supplement the planting area with some form of nitrogen fertilizer. I add either fish meal, following the prescribed amount given on the package, or a few shovels full of chicken manure for each plant. I then set the plant in the ground at the same height as it was in the container if it's a 4-inch container or smaller, and a little above ground level if it's in a one-gallon container or larger. I pat the plant in place gently by hand, and water each plant in well to remove air bubbles. If I'm planting on a very hot day or the transplants have been in a protected greenhouse, I shade them with a shingle or such, placed on the sunny side of the plants. I then install my drip irrigation tubing at this time (see "Irrigation" below for more information) and then mulch with a few inches of organic matter. I keep the transplants moist but not soggy for the first few weeks.

Selecting and Planting Roses

Variety selection is critical when choosing roses for your garden. Select those that are the most resistant to the diseases that are prevalent in your area. Try to resist being enticed by those photos of gorgeous roses—they will not look gorgeous when they are covered with diseases. And you will not be able to eat the flowers if they are covered with toxic fungicides. Contact the American Rose Society, your local rose society, county agricultural extension agent, or locally owned nurseries for information on roses that are suitable for your area. Unfortunately, it is difficult to get roses tailored to your climate from large chain nurseries and building-supply firms, as they often offer the same roses nationwide. As a rule, some of the old varieties and most modern shrub landscape roses have far fewer problems than most hybrid tea and floribunda roses.

When you are planting roses, calculate how far each variety will spread and how tall it will get. Situate the short varieties in the front of the bed and the tall ones in back. Fungus diseases are the major problem when you grow roses, so it's critical that you give each plant plenty of room for good air circulation. (Note that the planting size for roses listed in catalogs is an average. If you live in the coldest part of a recommended zone for a particular rose, assume that the plant will be smaller than described. If you live in a mild-winter area, assume that the plant will get larger than reported.) After preparing the planting beds, dig a planting hole for each rose and add half a bag of well-aged steer manure (about one cubic foot) and mix it well with the soil. I add ¼ cup of epsom salts for strong growth at this time as well. (Epsom salts are available in supermarkets or drugstores.) If you are planting bare-root roses, mound the soil in the hole and spread out the roots evenly over the mound. The depth at which you plant them is determined by the climate you live in. In mild-winter areas the bud union (where the upper part of the bush was grafted to the rootstock) should be right at 1 or 2 inches above the soil surface level. In cold-winter climates place the bud union 1 to 2 inches below the soil surface level. (The colder the

climate, the lower the bud union.) Finish filling in the hole with soil and gently tamp it in place. Build up a small watering basin, and water the rose in well. Then comes my secret formula for success: I mulch with a 2-inch layer of alfalfa meal or alfalfa pellets, mixed or topped off with 2 to 3 inches of an organic mulch, such as compost. Alfalfa meal or pellets slowly add nitrogen and trace elements to the soil. (I buy my alfalfa meal, or the pellets, from the local feedstore. The pellets are sold as rabbit food.) Keep all mulch at least six inches away from the base of the rose. Drip irrigation is the best possible method of keeping roses watered, as it keeps the foliage dry, a critical issue with black spot and rusts.

Maintaining the Edible Flower Garden

The backbone of appropriate maintenance is a knowledge of your soil and weather, an ability to recognize basic water- and nutrient-deficiency symptoms, and a familiarity with the plants you grow.

Annual Flowers

Annual plants are growing machines. As a rule, they need to grow rapidly with few interruptions so they have few pest problems. Once the plants are in the ground, continually monitoring them for nutrient deficiencies or drought can head off problems. Keep the beds weeded because the weeds compete for moisture and nutrients. In normal soil, anise hyssop, bee balm, borage, chives, saffron crocus, arugula, calendulas, dill, cilantro, fennel, violets, and nasturtiums usually will not need fertilizer, but broccoli, mustards, squash, strawberries, marigolds, violas, and pansies usually need a light application of a nitrogen fertilizer such as fish emulsion or fish meal midseason if they are to grow well. Pruning is seldom needed, but removing spent flowers, called deadheading, will cause most to flower more heavily and give the plants a neater appearance.

Perennial Flowers

As a rule, once perennials are established, they require less routine maintenance than most annuals. Fertilizing is usually not needed for average soil that has been well prepared (though most will benefit from an inch or two of compost applied once or twice a year). Pests and diseases are much less a problem than with annuals. The major tasks for perennials are weeding, annual pruning, and mulching and winter protection in cold climates.

You need to weed to make sure unwanted plants don't compete with and overpower your plants. Be especially vigilant and look for perennial grasses, which if left in place will grow among and over perennials like lavender, daylilies, saffron crocus, pinks, and strawberries and obliterate them. A good small triangular hoe will help you weed a small area if you start when the weeds are small and easily pulled. If you allow the weeds to get large, then a session of hand pulling is needed. In perennial plantings, if you apply a good mulch every spring, the need to weed will be minimal after a few years as the plants fill in and the annual mulch prevents weed seeds from sprouting.

Many perennials, like lavender, rosemary, sage, and thyme, need a major pruning every spring to force them to produce new succulent growth, to keep them from overgrowing an area, and to remove winter damage in cold climates. In long-season, mild climates, further pruning midseason after flowering is recommended to prevent the plants from getting woody and sometimes splaying in the middle. Chrysanthemums need pruning in late spring and again in early summer to keep them bushy and to prevent splaying. Other perennials such as anise hyssop, bee balm, pinks, and daylilies need pruning after they bloom to remove spent flower heads and to look neat and tidy.

The less hardy perennials need winter protection in the coldest climates. In the fall, after the ground has frozen, apply a six- to eight-inch mulch of straw or composted material around the plants to insulate the soil and prevent the cycle of freezing and thawing that heaves plants out of the ground. It also prevents the plants from drying out in cold, dry weather when there is not enough snow to cover the plants.

Some plants can be grown in containers and brought inside to a cool, dry place and then taken back out to the garden after the weather warms up.

Rose Maintenance

The amount and type of maintenance roses need depends a lot on the variety. Many of the old roses and modern shrub roses need little care compared with the complex and time-consuming care needed by hybrid tea and floribunda roses, which have been bred for the show table not for the average garden. See the Encyclopedia of Edible Flowers (page 29) for some recommended rose varieties.

For further information, read some of the books listed in the Bibliography or contact the American Rose Society and other rose organizations (see Resources, page 103).

Everblooming roses, including hybrid teas, floribundas, and grandifloras, need the most severe pruning; do so when they are dormant in late winter or early spring. Many of the once-blooming old roses that are particularly nice for edible flowers are pruned after their flowering is over in early summer; as a rule, cut them back by one-third to one-half. Some roses, like 'Flower Carpet' and 'Belinda,' will need to be pruned only for shaping. In all cases, damaged, dead, or diseased wood should always be pruned. After you prune, always clean up the canes and all leaves and debris on the ground and put them in the garbage.

The following fertilizing regimen has given me great results. Every spring, after pruning and just before the roses start to leaf out, apply fish meal according to the directions on the package and ¼ cup of epsom salts per plant, diluted in 1 gallon of water. Then mulch each plant with two inches of alfalfa meal or pellets. Later, in early summer after the first blooming has finished, deadhead the plants, then feed them again with fish emulsion or fish meal. Gardens with acidic soil may need an application of lime every few years to raise the pH.

In late fall in very cold winter climates, protect hybrid teas, grandifloras, and floribundas by watering well, cleaning up all old leaves and debris under the plant, and mounding soil six to ten inches up the canes. Top off the mounds with a thick mulch. Remove this protection in early spring. Most hardy shrub roses will not need special winter protection.

Mulching

Mulching with organic matter can save the gardener time, effort, and water, and the process builds great soil. A mulch reduces moisture loss, prevents erosion, controls weeds, minimizes soil compaction, and moderates soil temperature—keeping the roots cool in the summer and preventing them from heaving out of the soil in the winter. The organic material adds nutrients and organic matter to the soil as it decomposes, and it helps keep heavy clay porous and helps sandy soils retain moisture. Applying a few inches of organic matter every spring is necessary in most garden beds to keep them healthy. Mulch with compost from your compost pile, pine needles, composted sawdust, straw, or one of the many agricultural by-products such as rice hulls or grape pomace.

Composting

Compost is the humus-rich result of the decomposition of organic matter, such as leaves and lawn clippings. The objective in maintaining a composting system is to speed up decomposition and centralize the material so you can gather it up and spread it where it will do the most good. Compost's benefits include providing nutrients to plants in a slow-release, balanced fashion; helping break up clay soil; aiding sandy soil to retain moisture; and correcting pH problems. On top of that, compost is free, it can be made at home, and it is an excellent way to recycle our yard and kitchen "wastes." Compost can be used as a soil additive or a mulch.

There need be no great mystique about composting. To create the environment needed by the decay-causing microorganisms that do all the work, just include the following four ingredients, mixed well: three or four parts "brown" material high in carbon, such as dry leaves, dry grass, or even shredded black-and-white newspaper; one part "green" material high in nitrogen, such as fresh grass clippings, fresh garden

A three-bin composting system

trimmings, barnyard manure, or kitchen trimmings like pea pods and carrot tops; water in moderate amounts, so that the mixture is moist but not soggy; and air to supply oxygen to the microorganisms. Bury the kitchen trimmings within the pile, so as not to attract flies. Cut up any large pieces of material. Exclude weeds that have gone to seed, ivy clippings, and Bermuda grass clippings, because they can lead to the growth of those weeds, ivy, and Bermuda grass in the garden. Do not add meat, fat, diseased plants, woody branches, or cat or dog manure.

I don't stress myself about the proper proportions of compost materials, as long as I have a fairly good mix of materials from the garden. If the decomposition is too slow, it is usually because the pile has too much brown material, is too dry, or needs air. If the pile smells, there is too much green material or it is too wet. To speed up decomposition, I often chop or shred the materials before adding them to the pile and I may turn the pile occasionally to get additional oxygen to all parts. During decomposition, the materials can become quite hot and steamy, which is great; however, it is not mandatory that the compost become extremely hot.

You can make compost in a simple pile, wire or wood bins, or in rather expensive containers. The size should be about three feet high, wide, and tall for the most efficient decomposition and so the pile is easily workable. It can be up to five feet by five feet, but it then becomes harder to manage.

In a rainy climate it's a good idea to have a cover for the compost. I like to use three bins. I collect the compost materials in one bin, have a working bin, and when that bin is full, I turn the contents into the last bin, where it finishes its decomposition. I sift the finished compost into empty garbage cans so it does not leach its nutrients into the soil. The empty bin is then ready to fill up again.

Watering and Irrigation Systems

Even gardeners who live in rainy climates may need to do supplemental watering at specific times during the growing season. Therefore, most gardeners need some sort

of supplemental watering system and a knowledge of water management.

There is no easy formula for determining the correct amount or frequency of watering. Proper watering takes experience and observation. In addition to the specific watering needs noted above, the water needs of a particular plant depend on soil type, wind conditions, air temperature, and the type of plant. To water properly, you must learn how to recognize water-stress symptoms (often a dulling of foliage color as well as the better-known symptoms of drooping leaves and wilting), how much to water (too much is as bad as too little), and how to water. Some general rules are

1. Water deeply. Except for seed beds, most plants need infrequent deep watering rather than frequent light sprinkling.

2. To ensure proper absorption, apply water at a rate slow enough to prevent runoff.

3. Do not use overhead watering systems when the wind is blowing.

4. Try to water early in the morning so that foliage will have time to dry off before nightfall, thus preventing some disease problems. In addition, because of the cooler temperature, less water is lost to evaporation.

5. Test your watering system occasionally to make sure it is covering the area evenly.

6. Use methods and tools that conserve

Baby lettuces with drip irrigation

water. When you are using a hose, a pistol-grip nozzle will shut off the water while you move from one container or planting bed to another. Soaker hoses, made of either canvas or recycled tires, and other ooze and drip irrigation systems apply water slowly to shrub borders and vegetable gardens and use water more efficiently than do overhead systems.

Drip, or the related ooze/trickle, irrigation systems are advisable wherever feasible, and most gardens are well suited to them. Drip systems deliver water a drop at a time through spaghetti-like emitter tubes or plastic pipe with emitters, that drip water right onto the root zone of each plant. Because of the time and effort involved in installing one or two emitters per plant, these systems work best for permanent plantings such as in rose beds, with rows of daylilies and lavender, say, or with trees and shrubs. These lines require continual maintenance to make sure the individual emitters are not clogged.

Other similar systems, called ooze systems, deliver water through either holes made every six or twelve inches along solid flexible tubing or ooze along the entire porous hose. Neither system is as prone to clogging as are the emitters. The solid type is made of plastic and is often called laser tubing. It is pressure compensated, which means the flow of water is even throughout the length of the tubing. The high-quality brands have a built-in mechanism to minimize clogging and are made of tubing that will not expand in hot weather and, consequently, pop off their fittings. (Some of the inexpensive drip irrigation kits can make you crazy!) The porous hose types are made from recycled tires and come in two sizes—a standard hose diameter of one inch, great for shrubs and trees planted in a row, and ¼-inch tubing that can be snaked around beds of small plants. Neither are pressure compensated, which means the plants nearest the source of water get more water than those at the end of the line. It also means they will not work well if there is any slope. All types of drip emitter and ooze systems are installed after the plants are in the ground, and are held in place with ground staples.

To install any drip or ooze systems, you must also install an anti-siphon valve at the water sources to prevent dirty garden water from being drawn up into the house drinking water. Further, a filter is also needed to prevent debris from clogging the filters. One-inch distribution tubing is connected to the water source and laid out around the perimeter of the garden. Then smaller-diameter drip and ooze lines are connected to this. As you can see, installing these systems requires some thought and time. You can order these systems from either a specialty mail-order garden or irrigation source or visit your local plumbing supply store. I find the latter to be the best solution for all my irrigation problems. Over the years I've found that plumbing supply stores offer professional-quality supplies, usually for less money than the so-called inexpensive kits available in home-supply stores and some nurseries. In addition to quality materials, there are professionals there to help you lay out an irrigation design that is tailored to your garden. Whether you choose an emitter or an ooze system, when you go to buy your tubing, be prepared by bringing a rough drawing of the area to be irrigated—with dimensions, the location of the water source and any slopes, and, if possible, the water pressure at your water source. Let the professionals walk you through the steps and help pick out supplies that best fit your site.

Problems aside, all forms of drip irrigation are more efficient than furrow or standard overhead watering in delivering water to its precise destination, and they are well worth considering. They deliver water slowly, so it doesn't run off; they also water deeply, which encourages deep rooting. Drip irrigation also eliminates many disease problems, and because so little of the soil surface is moist, there are fewer weeds. Finally, they have the potential to waste a lot less water.

appendix B
pest and
disease
control

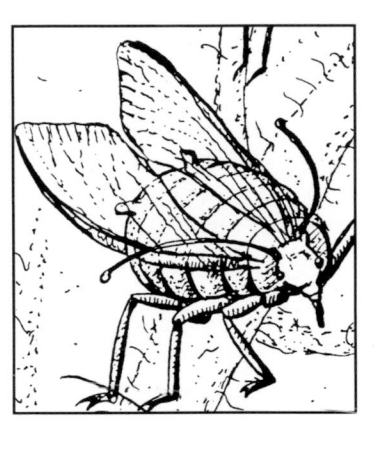

The following sections cover a large number of pests and diseases. An individual gardener, however, will encounter few such problems in a lifetime of gardening. Good garden planning, good hygiene, and an awareness of major symptoms will keep problems to a minimum and give you many hours to enjoy your garden.

While some edible flowers are as tasty to garden pests as they are to us, many edible flowers are herbs and have far fewer pests than the standard vegetable or flower garden. Deer and rabbits, say, are seldom interested in most herbs. Pest insects as well are seldom drawn to herbs, but in many cases beneficial insects are. Plants such as cilantro, dill, thyme, and fennel all produce many small flowers that provide nectar crucial to many beneficial insects at different stages of their life. Further, many flowering herbs like anise hyssop, chives, rosemary, sage, borage, chamomile, fennel, and lavender not only give us edible flowers but provide nectar and pollen to both domestic and wild bees. When you are aware of the insect world around you, you can help maintain the balance in your garden, and so benefit not only your plants, but all the plants in your neighborhood.

In a nutshell, few insects are potential problems; most are either neutral or beneficial to the garden. Given the chance, the beneficials do much of your insect control for you, provided that you don't use pesticides, as pesticides are apt to kill the beneficial insects as well as the problem insects. Like predatory lions stalking zebra, predatory ladybugs (lady beetles) or lacewing larvae hunt and eat aphids that might be attracted to your roses, say. Or a miniwasp parasitoid will lay eggs in the aphids. If you spray those aphids, even with a so-called benign pesticide such as insecticidal soap or pyrethrum, you'll kill off the ladybugs, lacewings, and that baby parasitoid wasp too. Most insecticides are broad spectrum, which means that they kill insects indiscriminately, not just the pests. In my opinion, organic gardeners who regularly use organic broad-spectrum insecticides have missed this point. If you use an "organic" pesticide, you may actually be eliminating a truly organic means of control, the beneficial insects.

Unfortunately, many gardeners are not aware of the benefits of the predator-prey relationship and are not able to recognize beneficial insects. The following sections will help you identify both helpful and pest organisms. A more detailed aid for identifying insects is *Rodale's Color Handbook of Garden Insects*, by Anna Carr. A hand lens is an invaluable and inexpensive tool that will also help you identify the insects in your garden.

Predators and Parasitoids

Insects that feed on other insects are divided into two types, the predators and the parasitoids. Predators are mobile. They stalk plants looking for such plant feeders as aphids and mites. Parasitoids, on the other hand, are insects that develop in or on the bodies, pupae, or eggs of other host insects. Most parasitoids are minute wasps or flies whose larvae (young stages) eat other insects from within. Some of these wasps are so small, they can develop within an aphid or an insect egg. Or one parasitoid egg can divide into several identical cells, each developing into identical miniwasp larvae, which can then kill an entire caterpillar. Though nearly invisible to most gardeners, parasitoids are the most specific and effective means of insect control.

The predator-prey relationship can be a fairly stable situation; when the natural system is working properly, pest insects inhabiting the garden along with the predators and parasites seldom become a problem. Sometimes, though, the system breaks down. For example, a number of imported pests have taken hold in this country. Unfortunately, when such organisms were brought here, their natural predators did not accompany them. Two pesky examples are the European brown snail and Japanese beetles. Neither organism has natural enemies in this country that provide sufficient controls. Where they occur, it is sometimes necessary to use physical means or selective pesticides that kill only the problem insect. Weather extremes sometime produce imbalances as well. For example, long stretches of hot, dry weather favor grasshoppers that eat gardens because the diseases that keep these insects in check are more prevalent under moist conditions.

There are other situations in which the predator-prey relationship gets out of balance because many gardening practices inadvertently work in favor of the pests. For example, when gardeners spray with broad-spectrum pesticides regularly, not all the insects in the garden are killed—and since predators and parasitoids generally reproduce more slowly than do the pests, regular spraying usually tips the balance in favor of the pests. Further, all too often the average yard has few plants that produce nectar for beneficial insects; instead, it is filled with grass and shrubs so that when a few tastier plants are put in, they attract the pests. Not only will the practices outlined here help you create a garden free of most pest problems, but, with the right plants, you can probably help eliminate other pest problems you or your neighbors have struggled with for years.

Attracting Beneficial Insects

Besides reducing your use of pesticides, the key to keeping a healthy balance in your garden is providing a diversity of plants, including plenty of nectar- and pollen-producing plants. Nectar is the primary food of the adult stage, and some larval stages, of many beneficial insects. The small flowers on the many herbs are just what tiny beneficial insects need. Many composites (flowers in the *Asteraceae* family), such as calendulas and the single-petaled chrysanthemums, also offer abundant nectar because their center contain numerous tiny flowers, each a source of nectar.

Following are a few of the predatory and parasitoid insects that are helpful in the garden. Their preservation and protection should be a major goal of your pest control strategy.

Ground beetles and their larvae are all predators. Most adult ground beetles are fairly large black beetles that scurry out from under lavender

or other perennials when you disturb them. Their favorite foods are soft-bodied larvae like root maggots; some even eat snails and slugs. If supplied with an undisturbed place to live, like your compost area or groupings of perennial plantings, ground beetles will be long-lived residents of your garden.

Lacewings are one of the most effective insect predators in the home garden. They are small green or brown gossamer-winged insects that in their adult stage eat flower nectar, pollen, aphid honeydew, and sometimes aphids and mealybugs. In the larval stage they look like little tan alligators. Called aphid lions, the larvae are fierce predators of aphids, mealybugs, mites, thrips, and whiteflies.

Lady Beetles (ladybugs) are the best known of the beneficial garden insects. Actually, there are about four hundred species of lady beetles in North America alone. They come in a variety of colors and markings in addition to the familiar red with black spots, but they are never green. Lady beetles and their fierce-looking alligator-shaped larvae eat aphids, mealybugs, and other small insects.

Spiders are close relatives of insects. There are hundreds of species, and they are some of the most effective controllers of pest insects.

Syrphid flies (also called flowerflies or hover flies) look like small bees hovering over flowers, but they have only two wings. Most have yellow and black stripes on

their body. Their larvae are small green maggots that live on leaves, eating aphids, mealybugs, other small insects, and mites.

Wasps are a large family of insects with transparent wings. Unfortunately, the few large wasps that sting have given wasps a bad name. In fact, all wasps are either insect predators or parasitoids. The parasitoid adult female lays her eggs in such insects as aphids and caterpillars, and the developing larvae devour the host.

Pests

The following pests are sometimes a problem in the garden.

Aphids are soft-bodied, small, green, black, pink, gold, or gray insects that produce many generations in one season. They suck plant juices and exude honeydew. Sometimes leaves under the aphids turn black from a secondary mold growing on the nutrient-rich how. Aphids are primarily a problem on roses, broccoli, and chives. A buildup of aphids can indicate the plant is under stress—are your roses getting enough water, or sunlight, say? Check first to see if stress is a problem and then try to correct it. If there is a large infestation, look for aphid mummies and other natural enemies mentioned above. Mummies are swollen brown or metallic-looking aphids. Inside the mummy a wasp parasitoid is growing. They are valuable, so keep them. To remove aphids generally, wash the foliage with a strong blast of water and cut back the foliage if they persist. Fertilize and water the plant, and check on it in a few days. Repeat with the water spray a few more times. In extreme situations spray with insecticidal soap or a neem product.

A number of **beetles** are garden pests. They include cucumber and Japanese beetles.

Cucumber beetles are ladybug-like green or yellow-green beetles with either black stripes or black spots. Japanese beetles are fairly large metallic blue or green with coppery wings. Cucumber beetles can be a problem on squash plants and may sometimes be found down inside the blossoms. Japanese beetles are often a problem on roses.

Beetles such as Japanese and cucumber beetles, if not in great numbers, can be controlled by hand picking—in the morning is best, when the beetles are slower. Knock them into a bowl of soapy water. Larger populations may need more control, however. Try a spray of insecticidal soap first; if you're not successful, use neem or pyrethrum. Japanese beetles were accidentally introduced into the United States early in this century and are now a serious problem in the eastern part of the country. The larval stage (a grub) lives on the roots of grasses, and the adult beetle skeletonizes the leaves of many plants and chews on flowers and buds. Certain species of beneficial nematodes have proved effective in controlling the larvae of Japanese beetles. Milky-spore, a naturally occurring soil-borne disease, is also used to control the beetles in the larval stage, although the disease is slow to work.

Nematodes are microscopic round worms that inhabit the soil in most of the United States, particularly in the Southeast. Most nematode species live on decaying matter or are predatory on other nematodes, insects, algae, or bacteria. (See "Beneficial Nematodes" below.) A few types are parasitic, attaching themselves to the roots of perennials, including daylilies, lavender, and rosemary. The symptoms of nematode damage are stunted-looking plants and small swellings or lesions on the roots.

To control nematodes, keep your soil high in organic matter (to encourage fungi and predatory nematodes, both of which act as biological controls). Some success has been recorded by interplanting with marigolds, which seem to inhibit the nematodes, and by using applications of beneficial nematodes available from insectaries. If all else fails, grow the susceptible plants in containers with sterilized soil.

Snails and slugs are not insects, of course, but mollusks. Marigolds, violets, calendulas, and pansies are among the plants they relish. They feed at night and can go dormant for months in times of drought or low food supply. In the absence of effective natural enemies (a few snail eggs are consumed by predatory beetles and earwigs), several snail-control strategies can be recommended. Since snails and slugs are most active after rain or irrigation, go out and destroy them on such nights. Only repeated forays provide adequate control. Planter boxes with a strip of copper applied along the top perimeter boards keep slugs and snails out—they won't cross the barrier. Any overhanging leaves that can provide a bridge into the bed will defeat the barrier. You will get some control by putting out shallow containers filled to within an inch of the top with cheap beer. The pests crawl in and are not able to crawl out.

Spider mites are among the few arachnids (spiders and their kin) that pose a problem in the garden. Mites are so small that a hand lens is usually needed to see them. They become a problem when they reproduce in great numbers and suck on the leaves of plants such as marigolds, roses, rosemary, sage, strawberries, and thyme. A symptom of serious mite damage is stippling on the leaves in the form of tiny white or yellow spots, sometimes accompanied by tiny webs. The major natural predators of spider mites are predatory mites, mite-eating thrips, and syrphid flies.

Mites are most likely to thrive on dusty leaves and in dry, warm weather. A routine foliage wash and misting of sensitive plants helps control mites. Mites are seldom a serious problem unless you have used heavy-duty pesticides that kill off predatory mites or if you are growing plants in the house. Cut plants back, and if you're using heavy-duty pesticides, stop the applications, and the balance could return. Serious infestations usually are controlled by using horticultural oil. For plants in the house, cut back foliage, wash it well, quarantine the plants, and apply refined horticultural oil.

If mites persist, discard the plants. (*Caution:* Always tend to plants with mites last, or wash tools well, as mites can hitch-hike on tools to other plants.)

Pest Control

Beneficial Nematodes (Entomopathogenic Nematodes) are microscopic round worms. Many nematodes are selective predators of certain insects, especially soil-dwelling insects. They can be purchased for use on various pests, including Japanese beetle and cucumber beetle larvae. Most beneficial nematodes must be mixed with water and need warm weather to survive. Be sure you are using the species for the pest you have and read the directions carefully for application. Since they are selective, they do not harm earthworms or other organisms.

Insecticidal soap sprays are effective against many pest insects, including caterpillars, aphids, mites, and whiteflies. They can be purchased or you can make a soap spray at home. As a rule, I recommend purchasing insecticidal soap, such as the one made by Safer Corporation, as it has been carefully formulated to give the most effective control with the least risk to your plants. If you do make your own, use a liquid dishwashing soap; do not use caustic or germicidal soaps.

Horticultural oils have been used for many years as dormant sprays on fruit trees. Today most horticultural oils are lightweight "summer" or "superior" horticultural oils that have been refined to remove the compounds that damage the leaves of growing plants. The more refined oil can be used on some plants to control pest insects and diseases; however, they do smother beneficial insects as well as pests. Follow the directions for summer concentrations. Always test the oil on a small part of the plant first, as some plants are very sensitive to oil sprays and will burn or lose their leaves. In addition, don't use horticultural oil on very hot days or on plants that are moisture-stressed.

Neem-oil extracts, which are derived from the neem tree (*Azadirachta indica*), have relatively low toxicity to mammals but are effective against a wide range of insects, including different types of aphids, cucumber beetles, and spider mites. They work in a variety of different ways. Check the label for more information. Neem is still fairly new in use in the United States. Although neem was thought at first to be harmless to beneficial insects, studies now show that some parasitoid beneficial insects that feed on neem-treated pest insects were unable to survive to adulthood.

Pyrethrum, a botanical insecticide, is toxic to a wide range of insects but has relatively low toxicity to most mammals and breaks down quickly in the presence of sunlight. The active ingredients in pyrethrum are pyrethins derived from chrysanthemum flowers. Do not confuse pyrethrum with pyrethoids which are much more toxic synthetics that do not biodegrade as quickly. Many pyrethrums have a synergist, piperonyl butoxide (PBO), added to increase the effectiveness. However, there is evidence that PBO may affect the human nervous system. Try to use pyrethrums without PBO added. Wear gloves, goggles, and a respirator when using pyrethrum.

Diseases

Plant diseases are potentially far more damaging to your plants than are most insects. Diseases are also more difficult to control because they usually grow inside the plant, and plants do not respond with immune mechanisms comparable to those that protect animals. Consequently, most plant-disease-control strategies feature prevention rather than control. Hence, the constant admonition to plant in soil with good drainage.

To keep diseases under control, it is very important to plant the "right plant in the right place." For instance, many perennials, such as lavender or sage, prefer a dry environment and will often develop root rot in soil that is continually wet. Check the cultural needs of a plant before placing it in your garden. Proper light, exposure, temperature, fertilization, and moisture are important factors in disease control. Diseased plants should always be discarded,

not composted. The entries for individual plants in the Encyclopedia of Edible Flowers (page 29) give specific cultural information.

Damping off is caused by a parasitic fungus that lives near the soil surface and attacks new young plants in their early seedling stage. It causes them to wilt and fall over just where they emerge from the soil. This fungus thrives under dark, humid conditions, so it can often be thwarted by keeping the seedlings in a bright, well-ventilated place in fast-draining soil.

Powdery mildew affects many plants, including roses, bee balm, lilacs, peas, and squash. This fungus disease appears as a powdery white growth on the leaves and causes new leaves and stem tips to curl. Whenever possible, plant resistant varieties. Make sure the plant has good air circulation, full sun, and adequate water. Powdery mildew is encouraged by fine films of water, such as from fog or high humidity, and discouraged by heavy flows of water. In some cases, it can be washed off with water from a hose; do so early in the day so the foliage will dry quickly. Spraying with refined horticultural oil, liquid sulfur, or baking soda every few weeks also controls mildew. (For baking soda spray, use 1 teaspoon baking soda to 1 quart warm water, with 1 teaspoon insecticidal soap to help the solution stick.) Test on a small part of the plant first. With some plants, such as peas and squashes, powdery mildew worsens toward the end of the season; it is best to just go ahead and remove the plant. Thoroughly clean up garden debris to help eliminate overwintering spores.

Root rot and **crown rot** are common problems for many perennials. A number of different fungi cause these rots; they are usually brought on by poor drainage, overwatering, or the crown (base) of the plant being covered by soil, mulch, or debris. The classic symptom of root rot is wilting—even after a rain or when a plant is well watered. Sometimes the wilting starts with only a few branches; other times the whole plant wilts. Plants are often stunted and yellow as well. The diagnosis is complete when the dead plant is pulled up to reveal rotten, black roots. There is no cure

for root and crown rots once they involve the whole plant. Remove and destroy the plant and correct the drainage problem.

Rust and black spot are fungal diseases that affect roses. Rust appears as orange spots on the underside of leaves. Black spot manifests as dark spots on leaves and canes; it can completely defoliate a plant. Plant resistant varieties if these diseases are prevalent in your area. Make sure the plant has good air circulation, full sun, and adequate water. Do not overhead water. Prune infected leaves and destroy them. Plants will usually recover. But in some cases, such as in cool, humid climates where black spot is prevalent, letting the plant defoliate often seriously weakens the plant. Spraying with refined horticultural oil, liquid sulfur, or baking soda is an effective control. Spray as directed in "Powdery Mildew," above, and repeat every seven to fourteen days while the problems persist.

resources

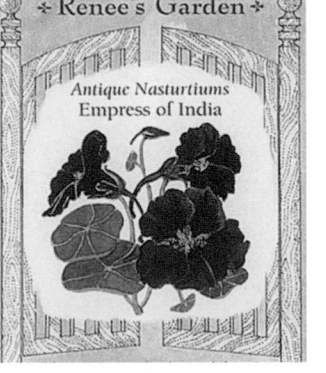

Sources for Seeds and Plants

The Antique Rose Emporium
10,000 FM 50
Brenham, TX 77833, USA
antiqueroseemporium.com
Digital catalog available
Great selection of old rose cultivars, species and disease-resistant roses

Chiltern Seeds
Crowmarsh Battle Barns
114 Preston Crowmarsh
Wallingford, OX10 6SL, England
www.chilternseeds.co.uk
info@chilternseeds.co.uk
Large variety of vegetable and flower seeds

The Cook's Garden
P.O. Box 535, Londonderry
VT 05148, USA
burpee.com
Superior varieties of vegetables, herbs and flowers

Evergreen Y.H. Enterprises
P.O. Box 17538, Anaheim
CA 92817, USA
evergreenseeds.com
Oriental vegetables and herbs

Seeds Savers Exchange
3094 North Winn Road
Decorah, Iowa 52101, USA
seedsavers.org
Digital catalog available
Heirloom flower and herb seeds

Johnny's Selected Seeds
955 Benton Ave,
Winslow, ME 04901, USA
johnnyseeds.com
Excellent selection of herb, vegetable and flower seeds

Harris Seeds
355 Paul Road, Rochester
NY 14624, USA
harrisseeds.com
Vegetable, herb and flower seeds

J.L. Hudson, Seedsman
Box 337, La Honda
CA 94020-0337, USA
jlhudsonseeds.net
Digital catalog available
Specializes in seeds of a huge variety of flowers and vegetables

Logee's Greenhouse
141 North Street
Danielson, CT 06239, USA
longees.com
Herb plants and seeds, ornamental perennial plants and citrus; many unusual varieties

Heirloom Seeds of New England
HeirloomSeedsofNewEngland.com
Seeds, flowers and vegetables

Nichols Garden Nursery
1190 Old Salem Rd NE
Albany, OR 97321, USA
nicholsgardennursery.com
Seeds and plants of herbs, flowers and vegetables; unusual varieties

Pinetree Garden Seeds
616 Lewiston Rd # A
New Gloucester, ME 04260, USA
superseeds.com
help@superseeds.com
Good selection of herbs, flowers and vegetables

Renee's Garden
6060 Graham Hill Rd. #A
Felton, CA 95018, USA
reneesgarden.com
customerservice@reneesgarden.com
Digital catalog available
Look for seed racks in better retail nurseries.

Richters Herbs
357 Durham Regional Hwy 47
Goodwood, ON L0C 1A0, Canada
richters.com
Digital catalog available
Most extensive selection of herb seeds and plants available to North America

True Leaf Market Seed Company
trueleafmarket.com
175 West 2700 South
Salt Lake City, Utah 84115, USA
Garden seeds, Growing Kits & Supplies - Organic & Heirloom Seeds

Select Seeds Antique Flowers
180 Stickney Road
Union, CT 06076-4617, USA
selectseeds.com
Digital catalog available
Specializes in species and antique flower seeds

Trees of Antiquity
20 Wellsona Road
Paso Robles, CA 93446, USA
treesofantiquity.com
Good selection of antique apples and other fruit trees

Stoke Seeds
PO Box 548, Buffalo,
NY 14240-0548, USA
PO Box 10, Thorold,
ON L2V 5E9, Canada
stokeseeds.com
Printed catalog available on request
Vegetable and flower seeds; large selection of annual edible flower seeds

Territorial Seed Company Store
20 E Palmer Ave, Cottage Grove,
OR 97424, USA
territorialseed.com
Catalog available on request
A great selection of natural fertilizers, soil amendments, and irrigation tools to keep your plants healthy and producing throughout the rest of the growing season!

Wayside Gardens
One Garden Lane
Hodges, SC 29653, USA
waysidegardens.com
Digital and printed catalog available on request

Plants of ornamental perennials and shrubs

Well-Sweep Herb Farm
205 Mt Bethel Rd, Port Murray, NJ 07865, USA
wellsweep.com
herbs@goes.com
Printed catalog available on request
No shipment of live plants to AZ, CA, OR and WA.
Extensive selection of herb seeds, plants and dried herbs

White Flower Farm Inc
167 Litchfield Rd, Morris CT 06763, USA
whiteflowerfarm.com
Printed catalog available on request
Carries a wide range of ornamental plants and a selection of disease-resistant roses

Organizations

American Horticultural Society
7931 E Boulevard Dr, Alexandria
VA 22308, USA
ahs.org
To purchase a copy of the Heat Map you may order online, or call (800) 777-7931 ext. 118, or email membership@ahs.org. Cost: $10 each

American Rose Society
P.O. Box 30000, Shreveport
LA 71130, USA
8877 Jefferson Paige Road
Shreveport, LA 71119, USA
rose.org
ars[at]rose[dot]org
Definitely worth joining as it can direct you to rose experts in your area who are knowledgeable about rose varieties and care for your climate

Canadian Rose Society
3125 Qu'Appelle Street
Victoria, BC V9A 1V5, Canada
canadianrosesociety.org
For only $20 (a year), you'll receive via e-mail 5 publications—4 newsletters and 1 larger 'Rosarian' in the fall

Flower & Herb Exchange
3094 North Winn Rd
Decorah, Iowa 52101, USA
seedsavers.org
Nonprofit organization dedicated to saving diversity. Members join an extensive network of gardeners who save and exchange flower and herb seeds

Royal National Rose Society,
The Gardens of the Rose
Chiswell Green Ln, St Albans
AL2 3NR, United Kingdom
rnrs.org.uk
mail@rnrs.org.uk
The Royal National Rose Society Gardens, also known as The Gardens of The Rose, are the gardens and headquarters of The Royal National Rose Society.

Seed Savers Exchange
3094 North Winn Rd.
Decorah, Iowa 52101, USA
customerservice@seedsavers.org
Digital and printed catalog available on request
Nonprofit organization dedicated to saving diversity. Members join an extensive network of gardeners who save and exchange vegetable and fruit seeds

Bibliography

Barash, Cathy Wilkinson. *Edible Flowers from Garden to Palate*. Golden, Colo.: Fulcrum Publishing, 1993.

Brown, Deni. *Encyclopedia of Herbs and Their Uses*. London: Dorling Kindersley, 1995.

Bryan, John E. and Coralie Castle. *The Edible Ornamental Garden*. San Francisco: 101 Productions, 1974.

Bubel, Nancy. *The New Seed-Starter's Handbook*. Emmaus, Pa.: Rodale Press, 1988.

Cathey, Dr. H. R. Marc. *Heat-Zone Gardening: How to Choose Plants That Thrive in Your Region's Warmest Weather*. Alexandria, Va.: Time-Life Custom Publishing, 1998.

Carr, Anna. *Rodale's Color Handbook of Garden Insects*. Emmaus, Pa.: Rodale Press, 1979.

Creasy, Rosalind. *The Complete Book of Edible Land-scaping*. San Francisco: Sierra Club Books, 1982.

Druitt, Liz, and Michael Shoup. *Landscaping with Antique Roses*. Newtown, Conn.: Taunton Press, 1992.

Editors of Sunset Books and Sunset Magazine. *Sunset National Garden Book*. Menlo Park, Calif.: Sunset Books, 1997.

Foster, Steven, and James A. Duke. *A Field Guide to Medicinal Plants—Eastern and Central North America*. Boston: Houghton Mifflin, 1990.

Gilkeson, Linda, Pam Peirce, and Miranda Smith. *Rodale's Pest & Disease Problem Solver: A Chemical-Free Guide to Keeping Your Garden Healthy*. Emmaus, Pa.: Rodale Press, 1996.

Hedrick, U. P., ed. *Sturtevant's Edible Plants of the World*. Reprint ed. New York: Dover Publications, 1972.

Hill, Madalene, and Gwen Barclay with Jean Hardy. *Southern Herb Growing*. Fredericksburg, Tex.: Shearer Publishing, 1987.

Hopkinson, Patricia, and Diane Miske, Jerry Parsons, Holly Shimizu. *The American Garden Guides: Herb Gardening*. New York: Pantheon Books, 1994.

Kowalchik, Claire, and William H. Hylton, ed. *Rodale's Illustrated Encyclopedia of Herbs*. Emmaus, Pa.: Rodale Press, 1987.

Lampe, Dr. Kenneth F. and Mary Ann McCann. *AMA Handbook of Poisonous and Injurious Plants*. Chicago: American Medical Association of Chicago, 1985.

Larkcom, Joy. *The Salad Garden*. New York: Viking, 1984.

McKeon, Judith C. *The Encyclopedia of Roses: An Organic Guide to Growing and Enjoying America's Favorite Flower*. Emmaus, Pa.: Rodale Press, 1995.

Ogden, Shepherd. *Step by Step Organic Flower Gardening*. New York: HarperCollins Publishers, 1995.

—. *Step by Step Organic Vegetable Gardening: The Gardening Classic Revised and Updated.* New York: HarperCollins Publishers, 1992.

Olkowski, William, Sheila Daar, and Helga Olkowski. *The Gardener's Guide to Common Sense Pest Control.* Newtown, Conn.: Taunton Press, 1995.

Oster, Maggie. *Flowering Herbs.* Stanford, Conn.: Longmeadow Press, 1991.

—. *The Rose Book: How to Grow Roses Organically and Use Them in Over 50 Beautiful Crafts.* Emmaus, Pa.: Rodale Press, 1994.

Peterson, Lee Allen and Roger Tory Peterson. *Field Guide to Edible Wild Plants: Eastern and Central North America.* Boston: Houghton Mifflin, 1982.

Philips, Roger. *Wild Food.* Boston: Little, Brown, 1986.

Proctor, Rob. *Annuals: Yearly Classics for the Contemporary Garden.* New York: HarperCollins Publishers, 1991.

Reilly, Ann. *Park's Success with Seeds.* Greenwood, S. C.: Geo. W. Park Seed Co., 1978.

Saville, Carole. *Exotic Herbs.* New York: Henry Holt and Co., 1997.

Schneider, Elizabeth. *Uncommon Fruits & Vegetables: A Commonsense Guide.* New York: Harper & Row, 1986.

Shepherd, Renee. *Recipes from a Kitchen Garden.* Felton, Calif.: Shepherd's Garden Publishing, 1987.

Smittle, Delilah, ed. *Rodale's Complete Garden Problem Solver.* Emmaus, Pa.: Rodale Press, 1997.

Walheim, Lance. *The Natural Rose Gardener.* Tucson, Ariz.: Ironwood Press, 1994.

Whealy, Diane. *1997 Flower and Herb Exchange.* Decorah, Iowa: Seed Saver Publications, 1997.

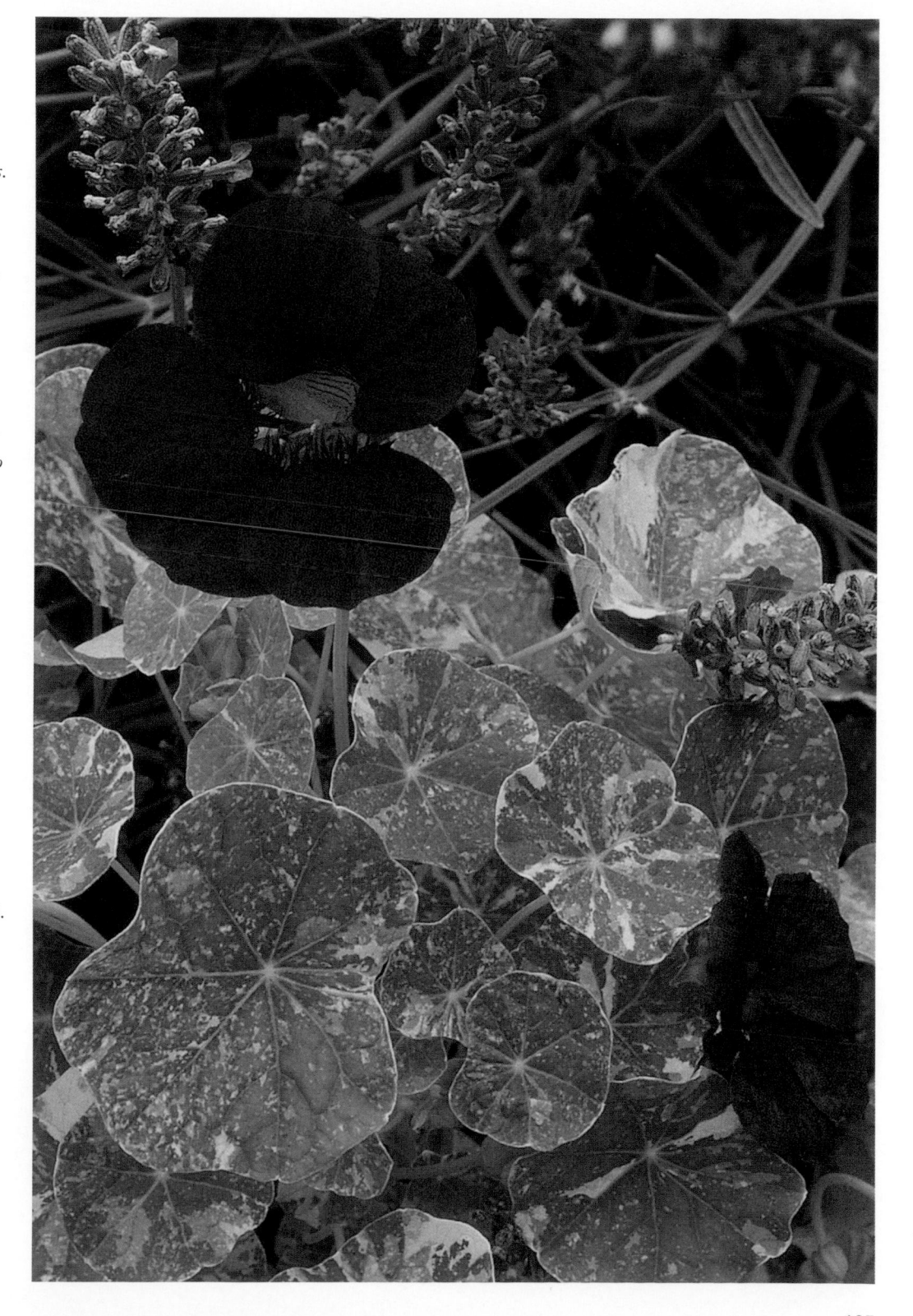

acknowledgments

My garden is the foundation for my books, photography, and recipes. For nearly twelve months of the year, we toil to keep it beautiful and bountiful. Unlike most gardens—as it is a photo studio and trial plot—it must look glorious, be healthy, and produce for the kitchen. To complicate the maintenance, all the beds are changed at least twice a year. Needless to say, it is a large undertaking. For two decades a quartet of talented organic gardener/cooks have not only given it hundreds of hours of loving attention, but they have also been generous with their vast knowledge of plants. Together we have forged our concept of gardening and cooking, much of which I share with you in this series of garden cookbooks.

I wish to thank Wendy Krupnick for giving the garden such a strong foundation and Joe Queirolo for maintaining it for many years and lending it such a gentle and sure hand. For the last decade, Jody Main and Duncan Minalga have helped me expand my garden horizons. No matter how complex the project, they enthusiastically rise to the occasion. In the kitchen, I am most fortunate to have Gudi Riter, a very talented cook who developed many of her skills in Germany and France. I thank her for the help she provides as we create recipes and present them in all their glory. I want to thank Carole Saville, who over the years has generously shared her vast knowledge of unusual plants and exotic cooking techniques; her knowledge of edible flowers is in evidence throughout this book. Alice Waters, of Chez Panisse in Berkeley, California, is to be thanked not only for opening her garden to me and sharing her many ideas on edible flowers, but for the continual inspiration she gives all of us who honor fresh garden produce. Tribute also goes to Andrea Crawford for trialing many varieties of edible flowers for me and sharing her studied evaluation.

I thank Dayna Lane for her steady hand and editorial assistance. In addition to day-to-day compilations, she joins me on our constant search for the most effective organic pest controls, superior herb varieties, and best sources for plants.

I would also like to thank a large supporting cast: my husband, Robert, who gives such quality technical advice and loving support; Nancy Favier for her occasional help in the garden and office; two edible flower mavens who are always on hand to share their expertise and contribute recipes, Renee Shepherd of Renee's Garden and Cathy Barash, editor of Meredith Books; a triumvirate including Jane Whitfield, Linda Gunnarson, and David Humphrey, who were integral to the initial vision of this book; Kathryn Sky-Peck for providing the style and quality of the layout; and Marcie Hawthorne for the lovely drawings. Heartfelt thanks to Eric Oey and to the entire Periplus staff, especially Deane Norton, Jan Johnson, and Sonia MacNeil, for their help. Finally, I would like to thank my editor, Isabelle Bleecker, for her gentle guidance, attention to detail, and thoughtful presence.

106